Africa Through Structuration Theory: Outline of the FS (Fear and Self-scrutiny) Methodology of Ubuntu

Jean Pierre Elonga Mboyo

Langaa Research & Publishing CIG
Mankon, Bamenda

Publisher
Langaa RPCIG
Langaa Research & Publishing Common Initiative Group
P.O. Box 902 Mankon
Bamenda
North West Region
Cameroon
Langaagrp@gmail.com
www.langaa-rpcig.net

Distributed in and outside N. America by African Books Collective
orders@africanbookscollective.com
www.africanbookcollective.com

ISBN: 978-9956-763-80-1

© Jean Pierre Elonga Mboyo 2016

Dedication

To my beloved and patient wife Marina and adorable children Verison, Fasia Cecille and Tyrell Elonga.

My wife and I set out to build the institution called family. When our children came along, each in the uniqueness, they transformed 'the family' and together our family is both the medium and product of everyone's presence. That is also what this book is about.

Acknowledgement

Some people set out to write a book. You can tell as you read the first chapter, come across the 'hindsight' reference in the fifth chapter and now the additional last two chapters in this new edition that the stages of publication happened as the thinking and writing process developed. Either way, other people around you play a part. I am, therefore, grateful for all the support I got from everyone when I needed my many drafts to be proofread, critiqued for readability, overall clarity and coherence. I will take the blame for any lingering speck of chunkiness. Although some have chosen to remain anonymous, I thank others at the end of the chapters wherever appropriate. All that is left is for me to thank my friends Vincent Asambom (critical friend through 1st edition) and Nicholas Oyugi (critical friend through 2nd edition) who, in our many a discussion, challenged some of my ideas and, in the process, enabled me to crystallise some of my thoughts. Immense gratitude goes to the anonymous referee for his/her constructive suggestions since the first edition and to Paul Close who, through his foreword, brings his wide readership to task to note the pertinence of the central issues being discussed here, and endorse the workability and originality of the proposed methodology of Ubuntu. I am also grateful to the production team at Langaa RPCIG for their patience.

Table of Contents

Foreword

Africa through Structuration Theory examines a debate of central importance to the African continent – how education systems can produce leaders to take its various countries forward from post-colonial and post dictatorial rule. It is an extended intellectual essay that would benefit from being read alongside its also recently published practical companion 'Trapped' (Elonga Mboyo, 2016a) that translates its developmental framework into practical activities that can be used to construct educational programmes in a variety of settings.

Africa through Structuration Theory is an entirely original piece of work for its combination of scope, conceptualisation, topicality and potential multiple audiences. Further, although its underpinning discipline is sociology, it will have relevance for readers from a variety of other disciplines, including politics and economics.

This second edition has responded to reviewers of the first edition who requested a more Afro- centric approach, clearer terms of reference and more discussion of implementation of the key 'FS' (Fear x Self-Scrutiny) framework presented, through revisions both within and beyond the 5 original chapters (reviewed by Kasanda, 2016). As outlined in the preface to this edition, chapter 3 now demonstrates more clearly how the interdependencies and collaboration of Ubuntu philosophy are an African version of structuration theory. Two further chapters have also been added. Chapter 6 discusses the status/ role of the African body in the expression of human agency and characterises different leadership practices in Africa that do not necessarily reflect the ideals of Ubuntu. Chapter 7 unpacks the central 'FS' framework by discussing the potential for change agency within it.

The original contribution to the field is in how this work builds on Obiakor's study of 2004. This posed two questions.

(1) What kind of educational philosophy can produce nationalism and patriotism in African leadership development and (2) How can the stability of such a philosophy be maintained? Obiakor's response focussed exclusively on structures at state level, analysing their weaknesses and proposing reforms. Like Obiakor, Elonga Mboyo's scope is continent- wide, but Elonga Mboyo offers a more complex analysis by bringing human agency into the equation and examining its symbiotic relationship with structure in a series of scenarios through Giddens' structuration theory. He also examines the methodological implications of researching an approach that combines subjective and objective perspectives, from collecting personal narratives to measuring effects of state policies, such as progressive taxation, on education reforms.

For Elonga Mboyo, human agency (ie of 'the people') is understood by the degree of FEAR in society, which is related to the degree of SELF SCRUTINY in its leaders of state structures. Taking us through 4 scenarios of high/ low fear and self-scrutiny he arrives at the characteristics of 'low fear' and high self-scrutiny which, he argues, are necessary for a healthy democratic society, while accepting in passing reference to 'Arab Spring' and what he calls 'the Singapore syndrome' that transition from authoritarian rule is not unproblematic.

The choice of Fear and Self Scrutiny as concepts for populating Giddens structuration theory is particularly appropriate to an Education /Leadership context against the backdrop of globalisation. As well as recognising more immediate fears for physical safety and emotional wellbeing Elonga Mboyo draws on sociologist Baumann's concept of fear in globalised society as loss of control where people 'feel incapable of averting or escaping the condition of being afraid' (Bauman, 2006:26). At the same time, the concept of self-scrutiny is relevant to debates around regimes of high stakes accountability in education systems across the globe, while as Elonga Mboyo demonstrates in his scenario of 'High Fear High – Self- Scrutiny', leaders can appropriate the seemingly unambiguous notion of The Rule of Law for their own interests. (see Lester, 2016, for an interesting further discussion of this).

I have followed Jean Pierre's work with interest since a spell as his doctoral supervisor a few years ago and commend this latest edition of his book to you for its original thinking and contribution to a topic of key social, economic and political importance, the future education and development of new leaders on the African continent.

Suggested further readings:
Lester, A. (2016) *Five Ideas to Fight For.* London: Oneworld Publications (Chapter 5: Rule of Law).
See this publication references for 'Trapped…' and others.

Paul Close
Email p.close@shu.ac.uk
Paul is a former course leader for MA Educational Leadership at Sheffield Hallam University. He has extensive experience of co-design of leadership development provision in the school-led English policy landscape and longstanding involvement in evaluation of leadership development for the National College for Teaching and Leadership in the era of national programmes. Paul's main research interest and contribution to the field is in agendas for the future development of so- called 'system leaders' in consultancy- based school improvement. In his earlier career, Paul was a Director of a consulting company specialising in multi- agency working in public services, and a Research Fellow in Organisation Development, an Advisory Teacher and a Head of English. Paul is an active reviewer and writer for a range of international journals in Educational Leadership and Management.

Recent publications

Close, P. (2016) System Leader consultancy development in English Schools: a long term agenda for a democratic future?. *School Leadership and Management*. Vol 36. No.1. April. 113-132.

Close, P. (2013) Developing political astuteness:- a leadership coaching journey. *School Leadership and Management*. vol. 33 no.2 April.178-196.

Close, P. (2012) Developing multi agency leadership in education. *School Leadership and Management*. vol.32.no.2 April. 123 -140.

Close, P. and Wainwright, J. (2010) Who's in charge?. Leadership and culture in extended service contexts. *School Leadership and Management. vol.30. no. 5. November. 435-450.*

Close, P. and Raynor, A (2010) Five literatures of organisation: Putting the context back into educational leadership. *School Leadership and Management. vol.30. no.3. July. 209- 224*

Close, P. (2009) From transition to transformation:-Leading the management of Change. chapter 5. in Mckimm, J and Phillips, K (eds) *Leadership and Management in Integrated Services. Exeter.Learning Matters.*

Simkins, T., Close, P. and Smith, R. (2009) Workshadowing as a process for facilitating leadership succession in primary schools. *School Leadership and Management. vol. 29. no.3. July. 239-51*

Simkins, T., Coldwell, M., Close, P. and Morgan, A. (2009) Outcomes of In School Leadership Development Work:-. A study of three NCSL programmes. *Educational Management, Administration and Leadership. January.37. 29-50*

Preface (1ˢᵗ and 2ⁿᵈ editions combined)

In the book chapter *'The movement towards democracy: global, continental and state perspectives'*, Wiseman (2002:2) makes the following remark about continental Africa: 'Africa is not a major actor on the world stage: in both military and economic terms it is extremely weak by global standard'. In this publication, I therefore seek to solve an enduring problem of poverty – whether chronic or transitory (Aliber 2003), underdevelopment and unfulfilled hopes on the African continent. I do so by drawing attention to leadership. In my view, such a challenging project cannot be successfully executed unless it is planted against the backdrop of a fitting understanding of how social reality is constructed. The structuration theory of Antony Giddens (1979; 1984), therefore, serves as a stepping stone to conceptualising various (African) historical facts with regard to both structure and agency. Analyses have led me to propose *duality of structures* as a solution to current leadership problems.

It is important for a brief narrative to be provided, just to remind ourselves about the nature of the problem, before I elaborate on how the specific issues discussed here interlink. Africa, whenever and wherever one starts looking at it, can be framed as a geographical location where the majority of people live in poverty despite the wealth around them. There is talk of renewed investment interests on the continent but, if they flourish, such success would be coming out on the heels of a devastating past. The paradox of 'poverty despite wealth' is common. In *West Africa Hosts Untapped Mineral Wealth*, the anonymous author (2010) describes Burkina Faso as hosting some of the richest untapped geographical wealth on the African continent. But due to a history of political instability, military coups, extreme drought and unfavourable investment legislation, it is not surprising that, until recently both majors and juniors alike have steered clear of the country' (54).

About Niger, it is remarked that 'the country has suffered a troubled political history and remains desperately poor' (56) despite its uranium and other minerals such as gold. About Liberia, the author mentions its iron ore:

> Iron ore exports accounted for more than half of the country's total export income and it was a major source of local employment. That iron industry was abruptly interrupted by civil war and continual fighting between 1989 and 2003. Violence left the war-torn nation crippled and poor, even by West Africa standards

And finally about Guinea-Conakry, the author highlights that the country is home to 30% of the world's bauxite reserves before highlighting its iron ore and gold deposits. Despite this wealth and the recent 2010 'democratic elections' in the country, peace is still precarious and the country still has to find a way out of the poverty that resulted partly from the authoritarian rule it was plunged into just after independence from France in 1958.

On the energy front, much still needs to be achieved. While the African population is predicted to grow by 71% by 2035, the increase in energy supply is expected to be only 38%. This is bound to trigger questions, given the fact that continental Africa has an abundance of natural gas and oil in northern and western Africa, an abundance of coal in southern Africa, and abundance of water resources in central Africa. Continental Africa can be regarded as one giant solar panel, and wind is plentiful in the arid desert and coastal regions. There is no shortage of energy resources, traditional or renewable. (Naidoo and Bacela 2012: 67-68)

The list of devastating stories is endless but there are some success stories too. The personal and institutional struggles against apartheid by the late noble peace prize laureate and former South African president Nelson Mandela stand out as one. However, more than a decade on since Wiseman (2002) put the first comment of this introductory preface into print, stories of dashed hopes and missed opportunities continue to plague the continent, so much so that the following observation by Antony Giddens is as valid today as it was then: 'in some African countries, living standards have fallen not just in relative terms but in absolute ones too' (Giddens 2002, xxvii).

The situation seems so hopeless that one wonders if Africa is predetermined to live in this way just as a dog is predetermined to eat bones. But here I am reminded of the Akan proverb (Ghana & Ivory Coast) that reads: 'Dogs do not actually prefer bones to meat; it is just no one ever gives them meat'. The largely youthful popular uprising that shook Tunisia, Egypt, Burkina Faso, the Democratic Republic of Congo (DRC)...can be seen as a show of Africa's determination to be recognised as a democratic and economic force on the world stage - moments when dogs refused to be fed with bones.

This publication attempts to offer a way out of the limbo in which we find ourselves, through a hopefully rigorous theoretical conceptualisation, which identifies leadership as a problem in Africa, offers research ideas and applies Giddens' structuration theory of duality of structures. Some might view my approach as abstract and idealistic. Firstly, when discussing matters that touch on the essence of a particular people (Africans in this case), philosophy and abstraction impose themselves, instead of it being a purely sterile academic indulgence unworthy of the seriousness of this publication. Secondly, the author sees it as a practical guide that uses concrete examples and effectively links abstraction to real situations. While the leadership examples of the likes of Nelson Mandela can presumably be regarded as prototypes of what the author is advocating, its future success admittedly depends on willing agents and structures that are honest enough to acknowledge the limits of old practices and give innovation a chance.

This book is therefore a conceptual enterprise that relies on secondary sources rather than first hand fieldwork in Africa. In other words, this is a duality-of-structures inspired agenda-setting conceptual analysis, which is largely based on a mixture of evidence from publications around the topics such as: politics, environment, democracy, conflict, leadership theories; methodological concepts; biographical illustrations; and the author's reflective diary. It does not depart from a tried and tested example of duality of structures to claim that this IS the way out of poverty. What it does, however, is provide (a) model analytical framework (s) for conceptualising current social problems/challenges in Africa and ignite a secondary-evidence based reflection on how leadership (and other related concepts) in Africa should be understood in order to revert the current narrative of poverty. To that extent, structuration theory CAN be a way out of poverty.

Based on the above understanding, it is expected that you, as a reader, would begin to wonder whether the argument this publication makes is either deductive or inductive. It is both and let me explain why I have come to that conclusion. Sidestepping individual preferences on the validity or veracity of either deductive or inductive methods (Tsang and Williams 2012), *Africa through Structuration Theory – ntu* can be viewed from a deductive point of view. It starts from a general sociological theory in order to understand a particular African context, even though the idea of a homogenous African context is somewhat problematic.

However, holding the argument (as this publication hopefully does), through the use of examples from various African countries supports the view here of a 'common' African context. Starting from an explicit theory (Structuration Theory) does not necessarily mean that the study is exclusively deductive and not inductive. Kimoyo (2008), Smeulers and Hoex (2010), to whom I refer later on, do not explicitly frame their study from Giddens' theory but, in reality, the studies' findings are based on an oscillation between citizens (agents) and governmental institutions' (structure) - struggles that led to barbaric acts such as those of the Rwandan genocide, for example. Since induction starts from particular examples to argue a (general) theory, one might accept structure and agency inferences from Kimoyo and Smeulers and Hoex's studies as one example. Not to view this publication as an inductive enterprise despite its integration of examples from across Africa is simply an attempt to subordinate secondary sources to primary sources arbitrarily.

The inclusion of examples (mainly from Africa), regardless of the order of importance that the reader attributes to either primary or secondary sources, should be enough reassurance that this publication is not based on assumptions which can be understood to be 'statements about phenomena that are accepted as valid without submission to tests of their validity' (Dixon 1977:119) or without proof (Oxford English Dictionary). That said, the book is divided as follows:

Chapter 1 '*African-Centred Leadership and the Theory of Structuration: a response to Obiakor*' presents one of the ways that has been suggested to resolve an enduring problem of poverty on the African continent. It analyses the arguments presented by Obiakor (2004) and, using Giddens' structuration theory, the chapter concludes with a slightly different approach to tackling the plight of Africans. The new perspective being suggested here requires to be seen not only as a reaction to a different approach but also as a philosophy in its own right, hence the second chapter, which serves as the foundation for this chapter and subsequent ones.

Chapter 2 '*Structure and agency dichotomy: an issue of trust?*' reviews structure and agency debate, brings some contemporary examples from Europe but mainly from Africa, and suggests that structure and agency have broken each other's trust and only a philosophy based on *duality of structures* could restore the broken trust between them.

Chapter 3 '*Duality of structures: a, not THE, methodology*' discusses the ontological, epistemological, ethical and other issues specifically related to Africa. In Chapter 1 'African-centred leadership and the theory of structuration: a response to Obiakor', I suggest that *Increasing self-scrutiny on the part of leaders and decreasing fear on the part of the population* are the dual indicators of a healthy exercise of duality of structures to restore the broken trust between structure and agency. In re-examining the African conception of ontology, epistemology and methodology, the author wonders whether Structuration Theory is, in effect, an 'authentically' African Theory. But if the analysis does not convince you as a reader, the author recognises it as an entrenched belief that anything remotely associated with the West is 'foreign' and therefore unsuitable in a different African setting. This issue questions this entire publication which effectively uses Antony Giddens' (British) social theory in an African context. The following chapter discusses this in more detail.

Chapter 4 *'Double de-contextualisation: a methodological myth or reality?'* engages with issues of how an African and others who may (or may not) be thought of as at the centre or peripheries of knowledge, apply theories that can be said to be bounded within some contextual structures, such as Europe/Africa, when engaged in research. The age of modernity has increased mobility and blurred boundaries. It is therefore essential that a repertoire of arguments is developed to justify the use of otherwise 'foreign' ideas on the African continent. There is an element of academic freedom argued not from a human rights perspective but from a scientific point of view instead.

Chapter 5 *'Higher education in the DRC and Sub Saharan Africa: an example of duality of structures in action'* discusses higher education in the DRC and Sub-Saharan Africa. Unlike the methodology chapter which sheds light on how to carry out research based on duality of structures, this chapter proposes a leadership and curriculum design framework for universities in the DRC and Sub-Saharan Africa, which stand as an example of duality of structures in action. It is only due to my professional and academic background in education that I discuss 'universities' here as an example. Otherwise, several other examples in fields such as health, judiciary, religion, business and media in various parts of the continent could be/have been investigated. There are undoubtedly such initiatives already and certainly many more will continue to address specific issues of poverty reduction from various perspectives in different fields. However, what this chapter/publication also does is to highlight the need for (a) converging conceptual framework(s) that would guide such actions.

Having so far approached the subject in a way that arguably equates human agency with human consciousness and provided evidence-based theorisation of what African leadership should consist of, two major questions have become pertinent and need answering: 1) what is the place of the human body in Africa and what is its role in the African agency that is dictated by Ubuntu? And 2) how close to or removed from the ideal Ubuntu leadership that I advocate are current African leadership practices?

In this new edition therefore, I attempt to respond to the above issues with 2 additional chapters.

Chapter 6: *'The Body Sociology and African'* examines various publications on the topic from an African perspective and tries to reconceptualise the literature in the light of the model developed in Chapter 7 to offer four ontological and methodological scenarios in which the African body finds itself.

Chapter 7: *'The FS (fear and self-scrutiny) methodology of structuration: a mapping of the field'* is the final chapter where I develop a methodology of structuration (of Ubuntu). This chapter methodologically maps out the ontological leadership spectrum in Africa. Sociologically speaking, it is hoped that the discussion will further render obsolete structure/agency dualism.

African wisdom has it that;

'If you want to go quickly (*or nowhere* – my italics), go alone. If you want to go far, go together' – African proverb.

The above proverb sums up the thinking proposed throughout the chapters, that of the need for interaction between structure and agency.

I hope to be read by all those who care about the plight of millions of Africans whose homelands have turned into prison cells they want so desperately to get out of. This volume can form the basis for discussions in many disciplines: philosophy, research, sociology, theology and many more. However, it is particularly aimed at African leaders at various levels, emerging academics in and outside their university auditoriums and the common man/woman who can digest the conceptual ideas on offer and begin to engage with them as a viable alternative to the status quo. It would be disingenuous to argue that ideas discussed here are transposable. However, given the reflexivity that we humans are naturally endowed with, it is possible to imagine that *duality of structures,* as interpreted here, *methodological dilemmas, de-contextualisation issues* and *duality of structures inspired leadership* of various fields, such as DRC and Sub-Saharan universities would be of relevance to someone in a non-African setting.

A major challenge, in my view, is the argument of applying a theoretical concept plucked out of its European setting to an African one. I pre-empt such a criticism by devoting an entire chapter to a broader discussion of the issue of (double) de-contextualisation.

However, it could be argued that de-contextualisation rhetoric is a discourse used by the African elites to position themselves as indispensable players in explaining, shaping and reshaping African social reality. There is a growing unease reflected even in the academic world where, for decades, as a discipline African Studies' 'primary motive and the logic that continues to propel it are aimed at decoding Africa and Africans for the world and not vice versa, still less the African world for African' (Olukoshi 2006, 539). The lack of internal debate among Africans only serves to feed into popular scepticism towards African leaders, academics and yet another publication on Africa.

Rather, scepticism from the masses (the agents who are supposed to shape and reshaped social reality) is the biggest obstacle that this publication could face. Africa is not short of learned and well intentioned individuals (elites) whose actions once in positions of responsibility have not always matched their spoken and/or written words. While such cynicism/scepticism is justifiably legitimate, this publication is not intended to be an application for an inexistent job/role for the author but rather for the cynical and non-cynical alike to take up the agentic job of shaping and reshaping their social realities. If I had to summarise, on basis of the author's passion rather than self-publicity, this entire publication in one sentence, I would say: 'this is your handbook for truly African cultural, economic, journalistic, leadership, political, religious, research, etc., actions'.

Préface

(1ère et 2ème éditions combinées)

Dans le chapitre intitulé '*Le mouvement vers la démocratie: perspectives mondiales, continentales et de l'Etat*', Wiseman (2002 :2) fait la remarque suivante à propos du continent Africain : 'l'Afrique n'est pas un acteur majeur sur la scène mondiale. En terme militaire et économique, elle est extrêmement faible'. Dans cette publication, je cherche à résoudre un problème persistant de la pauvreté - soit chronique et transitoire (Aliber 2003), sous-développement et déceptions dans le continent Africain. Cela se fait en attirant l'attention sur le leadership. Il me serait difficile d'exécuter un tel projet, sauf s'il était planté dans un contexte sociologique approprié. La théorie de la structuration d'Antony Giddens (1979; 1984), par conséquent, sert de tremplin à conceptualiser les divers faits historiques en ce qui concerne à la fois la structure et l'action. Par conséquent, l'auteur propose la dualité du structurel (la récursivité entre l'action et la structure) comme une solution aux problèmes actuels de leadership.

Il est important d'évoquer un bref récit juste pour nous rappeler de la nature du problème avant d'expliquer comment les questions spécifiques qui y sont abordées s'enchainent. L'Afrique, à n'importe quel point de repère, peut être conçue comme un lieu géographique où la majorité de la population vit dans la pauvreté malgré toutes les ressources disponibles. Au cours des dernières années, il y a un air d'investissement renouvelé sur le continent. Mais, si ces efforts aboutissent, un tel succès viendrait sur les talons d'un passé désastreux. Le paradoxe de la 'pauvreté malgré la richesse' est commun. Par exemple dans *West Africa Hosts Untapped Mineral Wealth*, l'auteur anonyme (2010) décrit le Burkina Faso comme hébergeant :

Une partie de la richesse géographique inexploitée dans le continent Africain. Mais en raison d'une histoire d'instabilité politique, coups d'Etat militaires, sécheresse extrême et de la législation défavorable à l'investissement, il n'est pas surprenant que, jusqu'à récemment, les grandes entreprises ont évité d'y investir (54).

À propos du Niger, il fait remarquer que 'le pays a souffert d'une histoire politique agitée et reste désespérément pauvre' (56) en dépit de son uranium et d'autres minerais tels que l'or. À propos de Liberia, l'auteur mentionne son minerai de fer:

Les exportations de minerai de fer ont représenté plus de la moitié des recettes d'exportation totale du pays et c'est une source majeure d'emploi pour les locaux. Cette industrie de fer a été brusquement interrompue par la guerre civile et de combats continuels entre 1989 et 2003. La violence a laissé la nation déchirée par la guerre, paralysée et pauvre, même selon les normes Afrique de l'Ouest

En ce qui concerne la Guinée-Conakry, l'auteur parle de 30% des réserves de bauxite du monde qu'abrite le pays avant de souligner ses minerais d'or et dépôts de fer. Malgré cette richesse et les dernières 'élections démocratiques' de 2010, la paix est encore précaire et le pays doit trouver une voie de sortie de la pauvreté qui en a résulté en partie par le régime autoritaire dans lequel il a été plongé juste après l'indépendance en 1958.

Sur le front de l'énergie, il reste encore beaucoup à faire. Alors que la population Africaine devrait croître de 71% en 2035, l'approvisionnement en énergie est attendu à 38% seulement. Ceci doit interpeller du fait que le continent Africain a

En abondance, le gaz naturel et le pétrole dans le nord et l'ouest, le charbon en Afrique du sud, et des ressources en eau en Afrique centrale. L'Afrique peut être considérée comme un géant panneau solaire, et le vent est abondant dans le désert aride et les régions côtières. Il n'y a pas pénurie de ressources énergétiques, traditionnelles ou renouvelables (Naidoo et Bacela 2012 :67-68).

Bien que la liste des échecs soit énorme, il y a certainement de quoi se réjouir. La lutte personnelle et institutionnelle contre l'apartheid de l'ancien président sud-africain Nelson Mandela se démarque comme l'un des exemples. Cependant, plus d'une décennie depuis que Wiseman (2002) a fait le commentaire utilisé pour commencer cette préface, les histoires de déception et des occasions ou opportunités manquées continuent à affliger le continent. 'Dans certains pays africains, le niveau de vie a diminué non seulement en terme relatif mais aussi en terme absolu' (Giddens 2002 :XXVII).

La situation est tellement désespérée qu'on se demande si l'Afrique est prédéterminée à vivre de cette manière comme un chien est prédéterminé à manger les os. Mais ici, chacun de nous doit se rappeler le proverbe Akan (Ghana et Côte d'Ivoire) qui dit 'les chiens ne préfèrent pas les os à la viande; c'est juste qu'on ne leur donne jamais la viande'. Les soulèvements populaires des jeunes qui ont secoué la Tunisie, l'Egypte, le Burkina Faso, la République Démocratique du Congo (RDC) ... peuvent être considérés comme un spectacle de la détermination de l'Afrique à être reconnue comme une force démocratique et économique sur la scène mondiale, des moments où les chiens ont voulu réaménager le menu et échanger les os pour la viande.

Cette publication tente d'offrir une voie de sortie à travers une conceptualisation théorique rigoureuse qui identifie le leadership comme un problème en Afrique et offre des idées d'application de la théorie de la structuration de Giddens. Elle pourrait être considérée comme un exercice purement intellectuel, abstrait et idéaliste. En guise de réponse, il faudrait d'abord reconnaitre qu'en abordant les questions qui touchent à l'essence d'un peuple (les Africains en l'occurrence), la philosophie et l'abstraction s'imposent au lieu d'être une indulgence purement académique et stérile. Deuxièmement, cette publication est conçue comme un guide pratique qui utilise des exemples concrets et en effet, rallie l'abstraction à la réalité. Le style de leadership de Nelson Mandela pourrait être considéré comme un prototype de ce que l'auteur préconise, mais sa réalisation avec succès dans l'avenir dépendra évidemment de la volonté de tous les acteurs et toutes les structures qui sont assez honnêtes pour reconnaître les limites des anciennes pratiques et donner la chance à l'innovation.

Ce livre est donc une entreprise conceptuelle qui s'appuie sur des sources secondaires plutôt que des recherches de premier degré menées en Afrique. Il offre un (des) modèle (s) ou grille (s) analytique (s) pour conceptualiser les problèmes sociaux / défis actuels en Afrique, déclencher des réflexions et tirer des leçons de leadership (et d'autres concepts connexes) pour enfin renverser et inverser le récit actuel de pauvreté.

Par ailleurs, l'argument central ici est déductif et inductif. Cette publication met en évidence un argument déductif dans la mesure où elle commence à partir d'une théorie sociologique générale pour comprendre un contexte particulier notamment l'Afrique, même si l'idée d'un contexte africain homogène est quelque peu problématique.

En outre cette publication met de l'avant un argument inductif. Bien que les travaux de Kimoyo (2008), Smeulers et Hoex (2010) entre autres, que l'auteur utilise un peu plus tard, ne font pas des références explicites sur la théorie de la structuration mais, en réalité, les conclusions de ces études sont basées sur une oscillation entre l'action (les agents ou les citoyens) et la structure (les institutions gouvernementales et autres). On pourrait inférer des études de premier degré de Kimoyo et de Smeulers et Hoex une récursivité entre la structure et l'action. Avec l'intégration des exemples concrets des autres auteurs sur l'Afrique et ailleurs, ne pas considérer les conclusions de cet ouvrage *'l'Afrique à travers la Théorie de la Structuration – ntu'* comme basées sur une entreprise inductive est tout simplement une tentative arbitraire de subordination des sources secondaires à des sources primaires.

Quel que soit l'ordre d'importance que le lecteur attribue à des sources primaires ou secondaires, l'inclusion de ces exemples doit rassurer que cette publication n'est pas fondée sur des déclarations acceptées comme valables sans (preuve ou) être soumises à des tests sur leur validité (Dixon 1977 :119). Cela dit; le livre est divisé comme suit:

Chapitre 1 *'African-Centred Leadership and the Theory of Structuration: a response to Obiakor'* présente une des façons suggérée par Obiakor (2004) pour résoudre le problème persistant de la pauvreté sur le continent africain. Il analyse les arguments qui y sont présentés et à l'aide de la théorie de la structuration, le chapitre se termine en suggérant une approche légèrement différente à adopter quant à la lutte contre le sort des Africains. La nouvelle perspective mérite d'être perçue pas comme une réaction à une approche différente, mais aussi comme une philosophie à part entière, d'où le deuxième chapitre qui sert de base à ce chapitre et la suite.

Chapitre 2 *'Structure and agency dichotomy: an issue of trust?'* fait la revue du débat entre la structure et l'action, apporte quelques exemples contemporains de l'Europe, mais surtout de l'Afrique, et démontre que la structure (les institutions) et l'action (les agents) ont brisé la confiance de l'une et de l'autre et qu'il nous faut la dualité du structurel pour restaurer la confiance brisée entre les deux.

Chapitre 3 *'Duality of structures: a, not THE, methodology'* examine les questions ontologiques, épistémologiques, éthiques et d'autres spécifiquement liées à l'Afrique. Dans le premier chapitre, l'auteur suggère que *'l'auto-examen en hausse'* de la part des dirigeants et la *'peur en baisse'* de la part de la population sont les deux indicateurs d'un exercice serein de la dualité du structurel pour restaurer la confiance brisée entre la structure et l'action. En réexaminant la conception Africaine de l'ontologie, l'épistémologie et de la méthodologie, l'auteur mène des analyses qui portent à suggérer un chevauchement entre la théorie de la structuration et l'ontologie Africaine (*..ntu*). Mais si une telle analyse ne vous convainc pas en tant que lecteur, l'auteur reconnaît que c'est en partie due à une croyance enracinée qui traite 'd'étranger', du 'néo-colonialisme' et en effet inapproprié dans le contexte Africain tout ce qui, de loin ou de prêt, a trait à l'Occident. Ce point fait planer le doute sur le fond de cette publication qui effectivement utilise la théorie d'Antony Giddens (Britannique) sur le contexte africain. Le chapitre suivant en discute de façon détaillée.

Chapitre 4 *'Double de-contextualisation: a methodological myth or reality?'* s'engage avec les questions de de-contextualisation. La modernité est caractérisée par une mobilité accrue et des frontières floues. Et pourtant il faut se poser la question : quelles connaissances et intelligences appartiennent exclusivement à l'Afrique et non à l'occident et vice versa ? Il est donc essentiel qu'un répertoire des arguments soit développé pour justifier l'utilisation des idées autrement dites 'étrangères' sur le continent Africain. Il y a ici un élément de la liberté académique soutenu pas du point de vue des droits de l'homme, mais plutôt en faisant recours aux arguments scientifiques.

Chapitre 5 *'Higher education in the DRC and Sub Saharan Africa: an example of duality of structures in action'* examine l'enseignement supérieur en RDC et en Afrique sub-saharienne. Contrairement au troisième chapitre dont la méthodologie éclaire la façon de mener des recherches basées sur de la dualité du structurel, ce chapitre propose un cadre de conception de leadership et de programmes d'études universitaires en RDC et en Afrique subsaharienne. Il se veut un exemple pratique de la dualité du structurel. C'est seulement à cause de son expérience professionnelle et académique dans l'enseignement que l'auteur discute les 'universités' ici. Sinon, plusieurs autres exemples dans des domaines tels que la santé, la justice, la religion, les affaires et les médias dans différentes parties du continent pourraient être (ont été) étudiés. Il y a sans doute de telles initiatives déjà et beaucoup plus vont certainement continuer à traiter des questions spécifiques de réduction de la pauvreté à partir de diverses perspectives dans différents domaines. Cependant, ce que ce chapitre (cette publication) fait aussi est de souligner la nécessité d'un cadre conceptuel convergeant qui guiderait ces actions.

Ayant jusqu'ici abordé le sujet d'une manière qui, peut-être, réduit l'agence humaine (l'action) au niveau de la conscience humaine, et fournit, avec preuves une théorisation pour démontrer à quoi consiste le leadership idéal Africain, deux questions majeures qui méritent des réponses me sont devenues pertinentes: 1) Quelle est la place du corps et quel est son rôle dans l'agence humaine (action) dans les sociétés Africaines qui se soumettent aux idéaux d'Ubuntu? Et 2) comment caractériser les pratiques actuelles de leadership en Afrique en rapport avec les idéaux d'Ubuntu que je préconise?

Dans cette nouvelle édition, je tente de répondre aux questions ci-dessus avec deux chapitres.

Chapitre 6: '*The Body Sociology and Africa*' 'examine de diverses publications sur le sujet du corps des Africains et tente de reconceptualiser la littérature à la lumière du modèle développé dans le 7ème chapitre pour offrir 4 scénarios méthodologiques dans lesquels le corps des Africains se trouve.

Chapitre 7: '*The FS (fear and self-scrutiny) methodology of structuration: a mapping of the field*' est le chapitre ultime où je développe une méthodologie de la structuration (d'Ubuntu). Ce chapitre met en exergue une méthodologie sur le spectre ontologique de leadership en Afrique. Sociologiquement parlant, j'espère que l'argument contribuera à rendre obsolète le dualisme entre la structure et l'action.

'Si vous voulez aller vite (*ou nulle part* - mes italiques), aller seul. Si vous voulez aller loin, aller ensemble' - proverbe africain. Cette sagesse africaine résume la pensée qui est proposée tout au long des chapitres précités, celle de la nécessité d'une interaction entre la structure et l'action.

Cette publication est destinée à tout le monde qui se soucis du sort des millions d'Africains dont les patries se sont transformées en cellules de prison. Elle s'adresse particulièrement aux dirigeants africains à tous les niveaux, des universitaires émergents dans et en dehors de leurs auditoires universitaires et hommes/femmes qui peuvent digérer les idées conceptuelles qui y sont proposées et commencer à s'engager avec eux comme une alternative viable au statu quo. Il serait malhonnête de prétendre que les idées discutées ici sont transposables. Cependant, compte tenu de la réflexivité dont nous sommes naturellement douées entant qu'êtres humains, il est possible d'imaginer que la dualité du structurel (*ntu*) telle qu'interprétée ici, les dilemmes méthodologiques, les questions de de-contextualisation et la dualité du structurel pour le leadership des universités en RDC et en Afrique subsaharienne inspireraient quelqu'un (e) dans un contexte non-africain.

Le défi majeur, à notre avis, est l'argument de l'application d'un concept théorique arraché de son contexte 'Européen' dans un contexte Africain. L'auteur devance une telle critique en consacrant tout un chapitre qui traite plus largement de la question de la (double) dé-contextualisation.

En revanche, la rhétorique de de-contextualisation pourrait être considérée comme un discours utilisé par les élites africaines pour se positionner comme des acteurs indispensables pouvant façonner et expliquer la réalité sociale africaine. Il ya un malaise croissant dans le monde universitaire où, pendant des décennies, les 'études africaines' en tant que discipline se sont assignées comme 'motif primaire de décoder l'Afrique et les Africains pour le monde et non l'inverse, encore moins le monde africain pour l'Afrique' (Olukoshi 2006 :539). L'absence de débat interne parmi les Africains nourrit le scepticisme populaire envers les dirigeants africains, des universitaires et encore une énième publication sur l'Afrique.

C'est plutôt le scepticisme des masses (les agents qui sont censés façonner et remodeler la réalité sociale), qui représente le plus grand obstacle au quel cette publication pourrait faire face. L'Afrique n'est pas à court d'individus compétents, bien intentionnés et éduqués dont les actions une fois dans les postes de responsabilité n'ont toujours pas reflétés leurs paroles et/ou écrits. Bien que tel cynisme/scepticisme soit légitime, cette publication n'est pas une demande d'emploi inexistant pour l'auteur, mais plutôt pour le cynique et non-cynique à s'engager dans l'action de modeler et remodeler leurs réalités sociales.

Chapter 1

'African-Centred leadership' and the theory of structuration: a response to Obiakor

Abstract:

Dissatisfaction with one system of organisation or governance can lead to calls for a change for the better. There are numerous such calls specifically aimed at Africa wanting, hoping and urging it to emerge and better the lives of its people. One suggestion that is represented here by accounts from the 2004 Obiakor article has been for Africa to recapture itself in a typical Hegelian cycle of opposites of structures or systems of governance. This chapter attempts to reframe the problem with African leadership using Giddens' duality of structures and proposes a slightly different discourse that should be given voice in the African leadership narrative and renaissance.

Introduction

This chapter uses Giddens' (1979, 1984) social theory of *duality of structures* to reconceptualise the narrative of renewal with 'intrinsic' African values associated with pre-colonial Africa, lost in the colonial era, and further alienated in the post-colonial time. It begins with a summary and then an analytical review of Obiakor's (2004) article which traces African leadership through the periods of pre-colonialism, colonialism, post-colonialism to post-dictatorship and advocates for an African-centred education that would produce 'patriotic' leaders and ensure Africa makes an irreversible entry into prosperity. The review is then followed by an outline of the theme of duality of structures within Giddens' social structuration theory, which is linked to

1

his views on modernity. His concepts equip my writing of this chapter with a theoretical framework to question and consider some of the pertinent issues that have so far remained unexamined. The section 'A new perspective for Africa using Giddens' structuration theory' re-examines the role that individual Africans would have played in the formation of their pre-colonial, colonial and post-colonial institutions. Reflecting on what needs to be done if the leadership of current and future institutions/movements/projects (states, African-centred education, African renaissance etc.) is to be successful, the chapter concludes by arguing that a cross-section or multi-fields engagement with social phenomena constructed through the interplay of structure and agency is what is needed.

Giddens did not develop a coherent methodological perspective for his structuration theory; hence, an *increasing sense of self-scrutiny* on the one hand and *decreasing fear* on the other hand are my experience-based indicators of the effects of such interplay and could serve as possible ways of testing the duality of structures in the context discussed here.

There is something that the reader needs to know before proceeding. This chapter was originally submitted for publication in an international peer reviewed journal. It was accepted initially and the comments from reviewers are presented below. It was then denied publication for the reasons that appear at the end of the chapter where the author shares his response before proceeding on to other chapters.

Reviewer(s)'Comments to Author:

Reviewer1: Comments to the Author: I say well done and congratulation for engaging in an innovative thinking to solve an enduring problem; and also for promoting integrative analysis of multiple perspectives. That's good scholarship. However, avoid using Eurocentric terms such as "tribal." Also, make sure that at least one (XXX) reference is included in the reference section.

Reviewer 2, Comments to the Author: This article deals with an important topic and is worthy of publication with a minor revision. The article needs a careful revision in order to improve its overall clarity and readability. There are mechanical issues and awkward expressions here and there.

As described above, here is the multiple perspectives' approach that seeks to solve an enduring problem of leadership in Africa:

Why Obiakor matters and what he says: a summary

Social media and academic work are awash with Africans bemoaning colonisation and what are believed to be its modern day mutations through globalisation, international bodies, and Western academies. Mentan's (2015) work, entitled *Unmasking Social Science Imperialism: globalization theory as a phase of academic colonialism* is just one such example. Convinced by such legitimate rhetoric, you and I can be forgiven for looking for inspirational practices of leadership, for example, closer to home. The chances of achieving such a noble quest become improbable when the reality on the ground is that of nationalistic oppression, as Mentan (2009) documents in *Democratizing or Reconfiguring Predatory Autocracy? Myths and Realities in Africa Today*.

Disillusioned by the current practices of our fellow Africans in power, a recurrent salvific suggestion has been to restore traditional African values. But just how do we go about it, what do we hope to find and how do we adapt that new knowledge to the world today? These are some of the questions that are yet to be adequately articulated. Obiakor's (2004) article 'Building patriotic African leadership through African-centred education' makes a contribution worthy of our attention.

Obiakor sees Africa generally regressing in its education standards, economies and political leadership, despite isolated success stories in a handful of situations (countries). This, according to the author, is due to the adoption of Euro-centred

3

frameworks. Those frameworks are not clearly articulated. However, in an attempt to resolve the situation, the author begins by bringing to our attention the assumption that 'the kind of education the citizens receive reflects the kind of leaders it produces' (ibid 415). He then goes on to recommend the revamping of the whole education system that would 'incorporate African-centred problem solving, partnership building, and collaboration and consultation' (ibid 416) as its building blocks. Africa's ability to change attitudes through its systems of beliefs and ideals hangs on a robust African-centred education.

The rest of Obiakor's article is essentially a historical retracing of events which brings him to the conclusion that the African traditional values to be enshrined in an African centred-education existed in 'precolonial Africa and were lost during the colonial and postcolonial periods' (ibid 416). Those values, according to Obiakor, resurfaced in the leadership of Nelson Mandela, Julius Nyerere, Nkwame Nkruma.

As we engage in a critical review of Obiakor's article in the next section, it is important that the views on African values, their presence and/or absence through the eras of pre-colonial, colonial and post-colonial do not go unquestioned and hopefully reframe what has come to epitomise the African narrative. With the reality of contrived collegiality (Hargreaves 2003), just how are we to understand collaboration here? Who is to collaborate with whom and on what basis? These are important questions in need of answers.

When paying tribute to Nelson Mandela, the American president said:

> ...we will not see the likes of Nelson Mandela again, so it falls to us, as best as we can, to follow the example that he set, to make decisions guided not by hate, never discount the difference that one person can make and strive for a future worthy of sacrifice (Barak Obama 6/12/2013).

The above extract is carefully worded. It recognises the 'unrepeatable' uniqueness of these great African leaders in 'we will not see the likes of Nelson Mandela again...' To that extent, those leaders had special traits that set them apart from the rest of us. The extract, however, recognises that (African) leadership is an art that can be learnt and developed: '...it falls to us, as best as we can, to follow their example...'

But how did these great African leaders exercise their leadership aimed at shepherding their nations to their 'true African-ness'? Was it just a matter of excavating those lost traditional values and reinstating them in the Africa of today? Are African education systems ready for the African-centred education that Obiakor and many others are proposing? The contention here is that, there is something much more central that needs to be articulated and through which African education and other fields can be understood. 'Education (*like leadership and others*, my Italics), in the African traditional setting cannot (and indeed philosophically should not) be separated from life' (Reagan 2005:62).

This chapter, and the entire publication for that matter, is an attempt to understand African life, whether modern or traditional. There is also a moral duty that requires us to engage in creative thinking in order to reverse the continent's on-going plight. This chapter begins a kind of pedagogy of African leadership ideals using structuration theory and I argue, in later chapters, for a rapprochement between structuration theory and African ontology (*ntu*).

Obiakor and the African-centred education for African-centred leadership: a review

Obiakor (2004) is just one in a growing list (Du Bois 1973; Foster 1997; Lomotey 1994; Murrell 2002; Rabaka 2003; Warfield-Coppock 1995 and Wilson 1992) of academics who focus their writings on African-centred education. Reference to Du Bois' (1973) definition of African education will be made.

This is essential in so far as it is rooted in African continental origins and 'values'.

To say that Obiakor (2004) is not impressed with African leaders at the time of writing his article is an understatement. He uses his breadth of knowledge drawing from different sources to make his central point about the need for African education systems to be African-centred, which would lead to the production of more patriotic leaders who would, in his view, do better for future generations. African-centred education is only a means to achieving the goal of patriotic African leadership. The intention here is not to unpack the ins and outs of what he proposes as African-centred education; this chapter focuses instead on, as implied in his article, the ups and downs of his goal: 'African leadership'.

'The institutionalisation of a pragmatic system of African-centred education that opens concrete rooms for African experiments and African experiences and fosters the use of African body, soul and mind' (404) is an ideal that Obiakor (2004) traces back to pre-colonial Africa. At that time, he argues, there was a pervasive sense of collaboration, trust, integrity, consensus, and amicable conflict resolution to name but a few. Looking beyond single practices, such as storytelling, the entirely individual acts of pragmatism were, it would seem, manifestations of what he calls the 'cultural continuity'. He cites the example of chiefs allowing their children to inherit their thrones, which only swerves to highlight the 'passive' role that Africans would have played in the shaping of their institutions. One could argue that this may not have mattered to the '*Ubuntu*' style of leadership (Mbigi 1997) which is generous, people-oriented and as Obiakor (2004:407) would put it 'tied to the apron string of traditional African culture'.

To apply the same logic today does matter, not least because of the numerous acts of unpatriotic leadership throughout Africa. The degree of what Letseke (2013:351) calls 'shocking and horrifying incidents of moral indiscretions' (violent crime, premeditated murder, rape, assault, homophobic attacks and police brutality) in South Africa, which could be extended to the rest of the continent, is a reminder that Africans can be active agents (albeit in a negative way as implied in Letseke's article) and, more importantly, that healthier articulations/expressions/manifestations of *Ubuntu* and African-centred leadership are necessary. It suffices to say that the narrative of pre-colonial Africa in Obiakor's article firmly grounds or subsumes the individual within the community and the temporal within the continuity. Individuals did not only act for themselves, they did so for the community, since they are an extension of the whole, of the structure.

The good times, or better still the seamless flow of the African 'cultural continuity', seem to have been interrupted by what he calls the 'Eurocentric intrusion', which, according to Onwudiwe and Ibelema (2003), continues to be felt today, though no longer known as 'colonisation' as it was then. This intrusion is presented by Obiakor as another system that superseded African cultural continuity. This system, on which Obiakor only focuses his critique on education, is characterised as leading to the satisfaction of European selfish ends, and destroying traditional African values and their gatekeepers (resisting rulers and chiefs) on its path to expansion. In what seems to be the continuation of his theme of Africans as individual moral and reflexive actors being lost in changing structures, Obiakor cites the example of traditional courts replacing African family collaborative structures in resolving problems. The mushroom courts were representative of a version of structures/systems that did not tolerate any deviant acts committed by individual. Another structure or institution cited is Christianity, which 'destroyed some great traditional values' (408). Once again, the individual (African leader in this case), wherever he/she stood, was absorbed by the institution in such a way that he or she became a puppet serving the interests of the new (colonial) structure.

The advent of an independent Africa, according to Obiakor, saw some examples of impressive leadership, but generally, the

7

promises of self-determination were short lived. For the best cases of post-colonial Africa, the author cites examples from Nigeria, Sudan and Tanzania for their daring authentic educational initiatives. The author does not state the goals in question but singles out Nigeria and Sudan as two of the nations that attempted to establish an education system with 'a national philosophy' (410). He then praises the patriotic move in Tanzania towards a socialist agenda whose ideology 'transcended virtually all social, cultural, economic, educational, and political levels of Tanzania' (410). While others might see these changes as Marxist experiments with Soviet backing, it does not mean that they are un-African.

One can then say that these initiatives were nationalistic and to some extent still had an institutional dimension. However, Obiakor presents them as singular and conscious attempts to write one's own destiny, rather than be part of a narrative that sees individual actions predetermined by a constraining (foreign) system. That, however, is still what happened according to Obiakor as colonial domination was replaced by African forms of (military) domination. The egoism of one tyrant meant that an entire nation and all its subjects had to dance to the tunes of the new version of domination and, like in the colonial period, the deviants were decimated. Idi Amin's oppressive rule in Uganda and that of Mobutu in the then Zaire are just two poignant examples illustrating a new devastating episode in the chain succession of subjects' subsuming structures.

In summary then, the narrative of the African leader and Africans as subjects that Obiakor eloquently and patriotically presents can be understood as one string of structure upon structure, which has at times, especially in the pre-colonial Africa, encapsulated the African spirit and, at other times, in this case the colonial and post-colonial, betrayed it. His optimistic, post-dictatorial/military Africa is, in my reading of his argument, yet another indulgent moment within the structure of pre-colonial Africa. The abovementioned phrasing of Obiakor's narrative should not be misunderstood as an antithesis to the

8

consensus surrounding the nobleness represented by pre-colonial values. Most of them, for example: the freedom bells, fighting corruption, democracy, self-reliance and skills-focused education for problem solving, partnership building, collaboration and consultation are based, it would seem, on the principle of human justice and, in a sense, are not exclusive to Africa.

The *Pedagogy of the oppressed* by Freire (1970), for example, can be understood as a Latin American version of a call for more patriotic leaders who would put social justice at the heart of their policies. Underpinning the pre-colonial values, one could argue, is the desire to humanise. On the subject of humanisation, Freire (1970:25) writes 'both humanisation and dehumanisation are real alternatives, only the first is the people's vocation'. Yes, this vocation can be culturally ring fenced and protected but it is, according to Freire, a vocation of *the people*, which I take to mean *all* people. Humanity belongs to all and it could be argued that all the conceptual ideas (Giddens' and others that are highlighted in this chapter) that help 'humanise' different groups, irrespective of their cultural backgrounds, survive the bias of being another form of educational or intellectual neo-colonialism (Altbach 1971). To return to the main point, Obiakor's pursuit of a (pre-colonial) structural rediscovery leads him to argue that:

> '...Interestingly, these skills used to be evident during the pre-colonial Africa and were lost during the colonial and post-colonial periods' (416).

Writing in 2001, the then South African President Thabo Mbeki goes to great lengths to define the African renaissance by attempting both to strike a balance between a return to a pre-colonial structure and at the same time redefine its very self. Addressing his South African audience, he says 'the institution of traditional leadership can and should play a central role in the African renaissance' and goes on to say '...to speak of African

9

renaissance is to speak of the coming into being of a new African identity…' Justifying this rhetoric was the setting up of an 'African recovery programme' by African leaders to eradicate poverty across the continent. It is worth noting that, despite this initiative coming earlier than the writing of his article, it did not stop Obiakor (2004) from deploring what he saw as 'unpatriotic' leadership. Nevertheless, while Obiakor's African-centred education is a different initiative from the African recovery program of Mbeki, in that the first produces great patriotic leaders and the second is a step towards the renewal of the new identity, they are both articulations of institutionalised vehicles for structural values to be transmitted. More efforts need to be made then to understand, define and promote the interactions that individual subjects or citizens have had with previous structures and will have with the new suggested structures. Simply appealing to people to commit to new structures that supposedly have their interests at heart (be it African-centred education or African recovery programs), without giving voice to an agentic African narrative, seems to me short of a credible renaissance and (African-centred) leadership.

For the purpose of my argument, the next section outlines Giddens' (1979) theory of structuration and appreciates its relevance in the context of a more globalised world or high modernity (Giddens 1984). This leads to posing some pertinent questions regarding the place of African citizens in what I deem to be a one-sided structuration narrative. This section refers to Giddens' original texts as well as other commentaries (Archer 1995; Elster 1982; Fuchs 2003; Jones and Karsten 2008; and Stones 2005) that faithfully elucidate on and scrutinise his rather complex theory.

Giddens' theory of structuration

Giddens (1979), like Bourdieu (1984) for example, is concerned with the dichotomisation of structure and human agency in the shaping of social reality. He dislikes functionalism which places the system's needs over and above the needs of individuals. Giddens' call to social theorists then, and I would argue that the same call applies to those attempting to understand social phenomena with an economic, political, cultural and ethical interest, is to bear in mind that,

> The pressing task facing social theory today is not to further the conceptual elimination of the subject, but on the contrary, to promote a *recovery of the subject* without lapsing into subjectivism. Such a recovery, I wish to argue involves a grasp of what cannot be said (or thought) as *practice* (Giddens 1979:44).

In an attempt to provide a coherent social theory that is not caught up in the logic of either functionalism or interpretism, either structure or agency, Giddens proposes that social environment be viewed in a *duality of structures*. This concept is essential in understanding the interplay that Giddens envisages between structure and agency and therefore avoiding the imperialism of the subject advocated by the interpretive sociologists against that of the social order vehemently defended by the functionalists/structuralists (Fuchs 2003). He first sees societies as having rules and resources. The duality of such structural properties is felt in that they both constrain and enable. One of the most succinct ways of explaining the constraining and enabling process of social phenomena is set out by Jones and Karsten (2008). They argue that:

> Giddens proposes that structure and agency are a mutually constitutive duality. Thus social phenomena are not the product of *either* structure *or* agency, but of both. Social structure is not independent of agency, nor is agency independent of structure. Rather, human agents draw on social structures in their actions, and at the same time these actions serve to produce and reproduce social structure (129).

In this way of thinking, there is room to argue that the past could have been (and the future could be) different, as structures get reproduced through the instantaneous actions of individuals. This dialectic between structure and agency and its focus on the here and now has come under criticism. The first is not so much of a criticism, as Giddens is aware of the fact that the natural world has a constraining hold on individuals without giving the actors any enabling option. To illustrate this, one has only to imagine that one cannot walk across the Atlantic Ocean without drowning. Metaphorically and in the context of the social world then, pre-existent social actions (Archer 1995) can define the conditions within which one acts in the present. These pre-existent social actions (elected or imposed as laws and norms) are, according to Stones (2005), what Archer refers to as external structures and Giddens calls the objective existent. They both refer to structural properties that the individual cannot change.

To further clarify structuration theory, Stones (2005:20) argues that the pre-existent social actions or norms are not to be thought of in a causal process, where there is a 'sequence in terms of a discrete structural moment being succeeded by a discrete and entirely separate moment of agency, which is then succeeded by another discrete moment of structure, and so on'. With regard to the ability of individual agents to change their environment in the on-going dialectic of duality of structures, Giddens distinguishes between the constraint as normative sanction and as structural constraint (Stones 2005). In the former, rules and norms may build pre-existent conditions that are resistant to change. However, they, especially inequitable rules, 'are not experienced that way as they don't prevent her from doing what she wants to do – they may even enable, facilitate desired actions' (Stones 2005:59) though gatekeepers of structures may impose punishment on the transgressors. A bit like some aspects of the natural world that cannot be changed (the example of 'not being able to walk across the Atlantic ocean without drowning' has been used here while Giddens uses the example of 'a person not being able to walk through a wall'), the latter, structural constraints, refers to engagement, contract or even norms that confront the actor as an external reality which cannot be changed, but that is only in as far as it is viewed as an external reality. It is worth wondering whether, in social interactions, constraints as normative sanction are ascribed the same nature as structural constraints, and vice versa.

To summarise the argument, Giddens' structuration theme of duality of structures has highlighted a number of things. The first is the primacy of the duality of structures over dualism. This means that social phenomena are no longer to be regarded as an exclusive domain of either objective social structures or the individual subjects. Ontologically, objective social structures and individuals are now to be regarded as standing on an equal footing. Historically, the past, present and future are a mobilisation of structural resources by individuals who, in turn, reproduce structures. To elucidate on this point, Stones (2005:21) writes,

the structures, in a sense, must come first into the agents before they can be drawn upon. Agents have structures within them. Equally, structures – the perceived configurations of legitimate and illegitimate actions, conventionally accepted meanings, and distributions of economic and authoritative power – are seen both to have agents within them and to be the product of agents.

The recognition of individuals' agency is even more essential as traditional structures that would have guided individual actions dissolve as a result of globalisation and modernity through increased information technology. Skilled social actors able to reflexively shape and reshape the new institutions, in the context of what Giddens (1984) calls 'high modernity', are necessary.

Secondly, both Obiakor and I write with a social justice agenda, which is to emancipate and make human life more

13

liveable. A value-free historical interplay between social structures and individual agents, therefore, is not enough. Hence, the resources that constitute the social structures are both individuals' *responsibility* and an *opportunity*. A responsibility in that they (individuals) would have contributed to its existence and an opportunity since the resources can still be used dialectically to reproduce further structures and change the course of history for the better.

There are rules which can constrain but it is important to remind ourselves that, unlike the natural world that cannot be changed, we agree to engage with constraint as normative sanction, not because the social world imposes unchangeable structural constraints on us. The rules and norms as normative sanctions can enable and facilitate desired actions (Stones 2005:9).

There can also be a tendency when thinking about these concepts to conceptualise the interaction between structure and agency as an end in itself. The responsibility and opportunity element root the theory of duality of structures firmly on the central goal of critical theory, which is human emancipation. The next section uses Giddens' concept of duality of structures to reframe the African-centred education or African leadership discourse.

A new perspective for Africa using Giddens' structuration theory

It is now worth looking back before looking forward. Before attempting to outline a new approach in the African leadership narrative, in the light of Giddens' structuration theory, it is essential that a retrospective reflection is provided to affirm the centrality of the theme of duality of structures in the African leadership narrative.

One area of reflection is what appears to be the tyranny of various structures over individual emancipatory prospects. The historical turning points, right from the pre-colonial to the 'post-dictatorial/military' Africa, appear to be times when structures were ways through which to conceptualise individuals. In the pre-colonial time, individuals were at an advantage, which was lost in the colonial and dictatorial eras. The thinking seems to have been dominated by a tendency to replace what, in the eyes of colonial Europeans, seemed dysfunctional with pre-colonial values. Dissatisfied with colonialism, post-colonial 'unpatriotic' (to stick to Obiakor's terms) leaders saw to replace colonial values with another structure. It is, therefore, legitimate to wonder if Africa is effectively in an endless cycle of recreating the problems that she was dissatisfied with in the first place.

The view here is that it is possible to recreate earlier problems if no attempt is made to reframe the problems that the African continent has encountered thus far. As indicated above, the problem does not lie in a bad system superseding a good one, but rather in failing to recognise the role that individuals have played and need to play, by drawing on structural resources to produce and reproduce their social structures (Giddens 1979). Below are a few examples to illustrate this point.

A pre-colonial example

Although one of Fafunwa's (1975, 1976) goals for education in the pre-colonial time, as cited by Obiakor (2004:406), was to 'inculcate respect for elders and those in position of authority', this would not be possible if individual acts by Africans did not happen to produce what is referred to, nostalgically, as 'African values'. When placed in space and time, these values (or structural resources to use Giddens' terms) were produced by agents of that time and there is no guarantee that agents interacting with structures today would reproduce the same values as those of the pre-colonial era, unless one decides to defend a philosophy contrary to the one implied in Heraclitus' famous metaphor, which reads *one cannot step in the same river twice* (Johnson 2004). Hence, traditional African values were what they were because individual agents made the structures what they were then. 'No traditional societies were wholly traditional, and traditions and cultures have been invented for diversity of

15

reasons' (Giddens 2002:40). Let us use an abridged version of an African story as an illustration.

Desperate to raise a child of their own, a couple goes to see a witch doctor to help the wife conceive. The witchdoctor performs his magic and next the lady falls pregnant. Rather than conceiving a baby, she carries a monster instead. Sensing some strange things in the house, the husband is instructed by another with doctor to exorcise the wife and the monster finally leaves her.

The moral, and arguably the core of the African value system, is the idea that children are a God given gift rather than the domain of witchdoctors. We may seek to inculcate this African, and also ecumenical, value to future generations but the development of modern technological procedures such as IVF, that Africans may (or may not) want to use, for example, make a reframing of the whole narrative an essential enterprise.

While attempting to gain an understanding of how values in traditional Africa would have been and how they can inspire future generations, the focus should mainly be on harnessing better and healthier interactions between Africans and the institutions they help to create. In community cultures 'where a singular feeling (*reasoning or choosing* – my italics) self is not necessarily the primary axis of signification (Riessman 2008:2), highlighting the role of individuals may seem an unsettling proposition. Such a constituency need not worry since my argument, in the light of Giddens' theory, is not about a lapsing into subjectivism but rather making subjects take their effective role in the building (producing and reproducing) of social and communal structures. In societies that take pride in their traditions, 'becoming detraditionalised' (Giddens 2002:43) threatens many things, not least people's identities. The agenda of duality of structures, as used here, is not an attempt to erode and replace traditions, but rather to renew, rethink and get to grips, as it were, with real African values and traditions in order to guide actions for a better Africa. It is, therefore, inaccurate to consider African values without recognising the contribution

16

of everyone, albeit within the rules and resources available to them at any given time, the pre-colonial in this case.

A colonial example

As previously stated, this period was characterised by 'Eurocentric intrusion'. It had 'puppet' leaders. The term 'puppet' can be taken to mean brainwashed people who are trained to think and act as they are told without having a mind of their own. However, since the vast majority of Africans had a mind of their own (then), it is logically sound, and within the theory of structuration, to argue that puppets acted in accordance with norms they could not change for fear of sanctions. Such constraints, in Giddens' term, are constraints as a normative sanction and did not prevent individual agents from doing what they wanted to do, even to the point of going against what one must do. Inexcusable acts of cruelty of the colonial era will remain what they are/were and the thinking here is not of victimisation. It is rather about recognising the pivotal role that subjects play in the reproduction of societies and beginning to realise that new structures suppressing individuals are based on shaky ground.

A post-colonial or independence example

After citing the example of Idi Amin's unpatriotic rule in Uganda, Obiakor concludes by saying 'it might be reasonable to summarise that, during postcolonial period, education failed to emancipate the African people' (2004:412). What suffered, in my view, were not the African values that, as already argued, would not be the same today even if the colonial era had not happened but rather the place/role of the individual in the shaping of a society in which he or she was a proud agent.

It has been said earlier that the aim here is not to unpack what 'African-centred education' might mean. However, it is worth mentioning that the idea of education being used to determine the path that individuals would take, instead of promoting and empowering individuals to reshape their social structures, is rather contentious. Those who might want to develop Obiakor's idea of 'African-centred education' would then be faced with the task of clarifying where it sits in the continuum of 'education for the economic needs of a nation' on the one hand and 'education for its own sake/development of subjective thinking skills' on the other hand (Hodge 2012), or integrate both principles. An elaboration of the concept of 'African-centred education' is even more necessary, so that it does not become a perpetuation of specific power relations favouring the dominant societal classes (Bourdieu and Passeron 1990; Grenfell 2008) as the pre-colonial example mentioned earlier might suggest.

Du Bois (1973), for example, has advanced a theory of African education that could help to avoid the perpetuation of dominant classes. His work is primarily aimed at the education of African Americans in the United States. However, his theory of education is linked to the historical and geographical origins of African Americans, which, in my view, makes it somewhat applicable to Africa as a continent. African education is defined as involving a critical study of African as well as world history, critical cultural study and an understanding of vital present and future needs not only of continental and diasporan Africans but also of humanity as a whole (Du Bois 1973). Such a view of African education cannot flourish if structural and institutional values of the pre-colonial era, for example, are all that we are concerned with. The critical approach, advocated by Du Bois suggests that a different understanding of the unfolding of social phenomena is necessary. That it is not bounded but rather dynamic, interactive and globalised, which requires skilled social actors to shape and reshape modern institutions (Giddens 1984). It is the contention here, therefore, that validating 'African-centred education' can be considered only as an attempt to make a more serious point about reviving or recovering a healthy agentic force, which would rehabilitate societal structures.

Even assuming the argument that has been made so far can stand the scrutiny of its harshest critics, there is yet an unresolved question of how, in African contexts, one can concretely operationalise and get a feel of a duality of structures' inspired leadership. In general terms, its best concrete application would be felt when individuals and societies interpret and act on their social realities in a way that alienates neither one nor the other. There are, however, some small steps that can be taken, as discussed below.

Looking ahead: taking small concrete steps

An essentialist approach to African-centred education would characterise it as being able to alter the deep-rooted disposition of an individual making him or her act patriotically in a position of leadership. What this does is exclude the vast majority of people who fall outside of the affordability-based education, and sideline them from playing an active role in the duality-of-structures based construction of social phenomena. In addition is the question of whether formal education is a liminal stage, where new ideas about society get created, or a reflection of the unfolding social life (Hargreaves 2003). The position here is that, it is both. And in so far as it is a reflection of social life, formal education is only one of the many theatres, or fields' to use Bourdieu's (1993) term, of the duality of structures. A non-exhaustive list of other theatres could be hospitals, religious groups, associations, cultural groups, the media, governments, regional and international bodies. To bring all these fields into play, a cross-section engagement with social phenomena constructed through the interplay of structure and agency is what is required. And it cannot happen unless it is triggered by the leaders, whether lobbied and willing or pressurised, of all these theatres. This somewhat civil society tone may have Eurocentric origin but it is also arguably what would have characterised the vision of great patriotic African leaders such as Nelson Mandela.

From my experience of growing up in and visiting several central African countries and receiving a Western higher education, I am able to propose some perhaps early indicators or signs of a healthier engagement with the duality of structures, such as *increasing self-scrutiny* by those in leadership positions, accompanied by *decreasing fear* on the part of individuals. In an environment where politics is a dirty word associated with dishonesty, *increasing self-scrutiny* has to be done with *honesty*. And yet, it is almost impossible to penetrate the realm of 'people's intentions' for us to tell with any kind of precision whether or not they are being honest. *Decreasing fear* on the part of individuals then becomes the only reliable measurement of sincere increased self-scrutinising structures. These two elements are what should, theoretically, be the guiding force behind of not only the many national conferences, dialogues or other variations *'les concertations nationales'*, as well as truth and reconciliation commissions, but also the business of leading public institutions.

Some literature on truth and reconciliation commissions, for example, has focused on whether truth does actually lead to reconciliation (Gibson 2004). If 'truth' is not a given, then it might be procedurally worthwhile to invest some of our research energy into understanding whether structures allow (self) scrutiny and whether subjects would feel free enough to tell the truth that would shape and reshape their institutions (example: a more reconciled society). What has been missing in African literature, therefore, is empirical research based on the degree to which individuals have felt a sense of agency in shaping and reshaping their social structures.

How do the two indicators apply in the leadership of Nelson Mandela, held here as a prototype of structuration theory-*ntu*? There are many examples of his leadership where *increasing self-scrutiny* on the part of an institution led to *decreasing fear* on the part of the South Africans in a compressed time and space, and we hope that other writers, even posthumous biographers, will begin to enlighten the world with more examples from Mandela's leadership of institutional *increased self-scrutiny* and citizens' *decreasing fear*. We will, however, provide two instances that occured in a decompressed time and space, meaning there is a distance in time and space between the two examples that are evoked here.

Under Mandela's leadership, Archbishop Desmond Tutu oversaw the proceedings of the truth and reconciliation commission, which was an eloquent example of institutional *increased self-scrutiny*. This was not just about the institutions coming clean about the atrocities committed in their era but also a statement that leadership draws its strength from admitting its failure unreservedly and allowing citizens to have a say in the shaping of the institutions of the future.

Despite retiring from active institutional politics, Mandela's leadership continued, this time drawing more attention to the promotion of agents' (Africans') *decreasing fear*. As the founder or co-founder of a group called 'the elders', a body bringing together older state's personalities around the world, Mandela presented this body as one whose aim was 'to support courage where there is fear, foster agreement where there is conflict and inspire hope where there is despair' (Mandela 2007). From our grasp and analysis of the current state of play in Africa, it does not take a genius to conclude that those living in fear, and therefore in need of the support that Mandela was talking about, are the agents, the citizens.

However, the prospects of 'truth and reconciliation commissions', national conferences, dialogues or 'concertations', convened in the true spirit of Giddens' structuration theory, are slim if this miniature duality of structures is not replicated in the day-to-day affairs of, say, any governing activities. This is where my growing concern with information ministries on the African continent comes in. These government institutions feel more like internal or external self-defence and propaganda mechanisms, instead of being used as a means for self-scrutiny, for internal efficacy, and as an opportunity for citizens to shape and reshape their structures. Decreasing self-scrutiny in brutal regimes of post-colonial Africa does not help to decrease but rather increases fear amongst individual agents and perhaps creates constraints, as normative sanctions seem like structural constraints.

Conclusion

An analysis of Obiakor's (2004) synopsis of African eras from pre- to post-colonial Africa has led me to argue that the narrative so far has been essentially about a succession of different systems or structures of leadership, which bring structure and agency dualism to the fore. With an interest in understanding the role of Africans as actors in previous systems (pre-colonial, colonial and post-colonial) and redefining their place in current and future structures (states, institutionalised African-centred education, African renaissance etc.,) being put forward, a much more focused analysis, using Giddens' theme of duality of structures within his structuration theory, has enabled me to propose a different reading of African history. This reading locates the ups and downs of African leadership in the use or neglect of individuals' agentic force to shape and reshape their social and political structures, which need skilled social actors to keep up with continuous changes associated with the modern world. Challenging the essentialist view of education as a means to produce patriotic leaders, this chapter proposes a cross-section engagement of structure and agency, with *increasing self-scrutiny* on the part of leaders and *decreasing fear* on the part of individual citizens as methodological indicators.

Giddens' failure to develop a coherent epistemology and methodology to go with his ontological concepts (Stones 2005) does not help. However, the lack of a clear methodology does not diminish the relevance of his conceptual thinking that this chapter hopes to have been able to demonstrate, as well as engage with the challenge of identifying a suitable epistemology when debating similar ideas in similar contexts. Hence, researching people's sense of (decreasing) fear and their ability to (self) scrutinise institutions and societal structures become potential indicators of Giddens' duality of structures. Chapter 7

22

uses the concepts of fear and self-scrutiny to summarise the entire publication and outline what I call a methodology of structuration (of Ubuntu).

After minor revisions, the article was denied publication, for the following reasons:

Comments to the Author: Reviewer 3

Who is Obiakor? Why is he important? What did he say that is worth listening to? There should be a summary of his main points before proceeding; otherwise, the article and its significance remain confusing. The categories of "pre-colonial," "colonial," and "post-colonial" are very Eurocentric and need to be interrogated, especially in a paper dealing with "African-centredness." By the way, why is "African-centered" not defined? What does it mean to the author? There are too many "I" in this text, which gives the impression that the article is based more on opinion than research. Why not use a theory produced by an Afrocentric theorist, like Molefi Asante, instead of one produced by Giddens, who certainly did not African in mind. This article reads as a purely intellectual exercise. It would benefit greatly from engaging truly Afrocentric scholarship and building upon it with an eye on making concrete recommendations on how to improve our reality.

Reviewer: 4 Comments to the Author

Scholars of the same intellectual persuasion as the author of "African-Centered Leadership and the Theory of Structuration" are likely to reason that this article makes a compelling case for a re-orientation and Africanisation of the values that underlie African education in order to yield a set of leaders who would lead with a sense of patriotism. However, the paper seems to be weak on how this sort of almost revolutionary educational objective could be operationalized at the various levels of education in light of the well-entrenched and prevailing neo-colonial social orders on the continent. Perhaps, a discussion of the latter issue of "how" may become the subject of a sequel to this initial piece.

With the above reviews in mind, it is evident that this chapter offers something worth considering, especially in a world where solving problems requires freeing ourselves from a monolithic thinking of a zero-sum game called 'truly Afrocentric Scholarship' and embracing multiple perspectives as reviewer 1 seems to suggest. The first of the previous two reviewers seems to miss the point when he or she asks why 'African-centred' is not defined. Yet what the entire chapter does is to define 'African-centred' along the lines of the theory of structuration where the construction of social phenomena is based on the interplay between structure and agency.

It is also true, as suggested by one of the reviewers, that this initial piece sets the ball rolling for a sequel, not only to address the 'how' question (methodology) but also to discuss other issues, for example, 'Why not use a theory produced by an Afrocentric theorist, like Molefi Asante, instead of one produced by Giddens, who certainly is not African in mind' picked up by reviewer 3. Overall, this chapter can be viewed as reactionary in the sense that it is mainly a response to an article. Therefore, before other discussions are introduced, it is important to develop and apply *duality of structures* as an independent theoretical framework when talking about Africa. The following chapter attempts to do just that.

Acknowledgement: I am grateful to Dr Paul Garland for his critical readership and proofreading an earlier version of this chapter.

Chapter 2

Structure and agency: (an issue of trust?)

Abstract

Structure and agency have been, and perhaps continue to be, held at opposing ends of the argument about the nature of social phenomena. Individually, they can be said to refer to clear entities and are value laden. This chapter argues that the claim for primacy of one over the other can be said to revolve around the issue of trust that each of them assumes and assures of the other. That sort of approach only stands if the trust narratives of both structure and agency are faultless. With stories of broken trust drawn mainly from the African continent, a case is made for Giddens' duality of structures being the basis for a credible way to restore trust and get structure and agency working together.

Introduction

In *Realist Social Theory: The Morphogenetic Approach* (1995), Archer mounts a sustained and perhaps compelling critique of Giddens' duality of structures within his theory of structuration (Giddens 1979; 1984). One of the criticisms, that is repeated by Stones (2005:52), is the idea that structure and agency 'are mixed together and confused such that any analytical value possessed by the concepts in the first place disappears'. This chapter explores some analytical values that the concepts represent when thought about separately. It also highlights the role that both structure and agency have played in diminishing their credibility vis-à-vis each other, hence the idea of 'crisis of trust' that appears later in this chapter. In the changing economic, environmental, social, educational, and political climate, the thinking is pushed further to focus on the value, not the alleged confusion, which could be borne out of the very fact of mixing the two concepts.

Structure:

The concept of 'structure' has been at the heart of ideological schools of thought, such as functionalism, structural functionalism, structuralism and post-structuralism. The aim here is neither to engage in a systematic historical development of the concept as articulated by Saussure, Lévi-Strauss, Derrida, Wittgenstein, etc., nor to provide a straightforward and simple explanation of such an elusive concept (Sewell 1992). However many unpalatable versions of 'structure' there may be, it is necessary to revisit certain reifications of the term in order to provide at least a basic understanding of what the concept 'structure' signifies. In this respect, it might be easier to conceptualise 'structure' as a hard, material, patterning mechanism that has a life of its own and governs a series of other transient and individual happenings. It is the immutable stability that not only transcends all but also within which everything fits. Whether that is a radicalised or basic version of functionalism or structuralism, it at least provides us with a starting point to begin identifying and naming various structures within everyday life. Borrowing from Durkheim's idea of *social facts* (1952), society within which individuals are members, culture as 'a pattern of basic assumptions that a given group has invented, discovered, or developed...' (Schein 1984:6), and language, can be viewed as structural entities.

Structuralism has its critics. Saussure's theory of language, for example, overturns the thinking that there is structure especially in language and is reported to have concluded that 'there is no natural or necessary connection between words (signifiers) and the concepts of the things to which they refer (that which is signified). Their relationship is arbitrary' (Hatch and Cunliffe 2013:41)

Giddens, however, has identified some values that the concept of 'structure' has brought. A more extensive discussion of these benefits of structuralism can be found in *Central Problems in Social Theory* (Giddens 1974). Intending to make a different kind of argument (the bracketed part of the title of this chapter *'an issue of trust?'*), this chapter will outline those advantages without much emphasis on their limitations, those which Giddens was keen to point out in order to make the case for his theory of *duality of structure*. For Giddens then, structuralism as a movement has made some significant contributions. When looking at the historicity of structuralist thinking, there is recognition of a temporal dimension within structuration. It represents the foundation of the theory of social reproduction, which links to the recursive properties that the structures or 'virtual systems' have come to be. There is an attempt to de-centre the subject as well as to transcend object/subject dualism, which Giddens cautions must be effectively done in a duality of structures. The final contribution that Giddens identifies is the analysis of the value of cultural objects. The view that nation states can be counted as cultural objects and the structural value this brings about is illustrated below.

Before we do that, it is important to remind ourselves of the social stabilising power that structures had in African (traditional) society. Contrary to what some Western scholars would say, Udokang (2014) traces the stability, order and harmony that African communal life had on the lives of individuals. Udokang uses two quotations to highlight the benefit of structure in African traditional societies:

> There exist many laws, customs, set forms of behaviour, regulations, rules, observances and taboos constituting the moral code and ethics of a given community or society. Any breach of this code of behaviour is considered evil, wrong or bad, for it is an injury or destruction to the accepted social order and peace... (Mbiti 1969:205).

27

Breaches were not only considered bad, they were severely punished as the following quotes shows:

Africans have traditionally been very conscious of the social dimension of morality. Morality is always seen in the social context. Hence any serious violation of the moral order has a social aspect which involves serious social consequences. The whole society is affected, for every evil act is an anti-social act which has adverse effects on the whole community (Tempels 1959:45).

By the end of colonialism and the wave of independence across the African continent in the 1960s (Thomson 2004), the independent states and their subsequent governments would have been (and arguably are still being) held as cultural objects for various individuals. Alluding to Anderson's (1991) idea of 'imagined communities', Thomson (2004) goes on to make a point that underpins the argument here about states, nations or, more precisely African nationalism after independence being cultural objects with a structural significance. He sums up the structural mood with the following:

Using interpretations of the past and symbols such as flags, anthems and ceremonies, the people of the nation generate social cohesion based on their shared national values and way of life. In this sense, individuals gain psychological and material protection from a sense of belonging. What is more, this security can be greatly enhanced if the nation is united with political power. This is where the idea of nationalism comes to the fore (35).

Hence, a further advantage of structures in this context is that they can become the embodiment of individuals' aspirations at the start of a new dawn, as some would refer to the years of African political independence. There is, however, the need now to explore what agency is all about.

Agency:

The subjectivism of the agents is 'exemplified by philosophers like Sartre and sociologists like Schutz' (Chandler 2013). When we think about agency; action, rationality, and emotions of individuals are the defining factors of social phenomena. Social interactions are not a pre-determined straight jacket for individuals to fit into. The focus here is on the subject, which could lead to what Cotterrell (2011:6), drawing on Durkheim (1975b), calls an 'unconditional respect for the dignity and autonomy of all individuals by virtue of their common humanity'. There is an element of voluntarism that determines social reality. Giddens treats agency, not as the sum total of discrete actions but a continuous flow of conduct. There is an assumed understanding that individuals can be trusted to determine structures and not the other way round. This, however, is not the case for all schools of thought that underline human actions. One of its most full-blown versions is in the form of rational choice theory. Here, individuals are considered free, calculating and egotistic in their motives to engage in social interactions (Denzin 1990).

One of the benefits of rational choice theory is the self-interest that is its own explanation needing no further clarification. However, as Boudon (1998) explains, the contradictions in different individual choices and the admission that actions can be non-instrumental question the very claims of the theory. More importantly for the purpose of the argument here, the egotistic dimension that could tear through structures borne out by individuals' actions shakes any trace of trust upon which any systems based on individuals' actions stand, in the face of the proponents of structuralism.

The literature from African scholars is conspicuously silent about the active role of agency (individuals). However, this is understandable if one makes a deliberate decision to champion structure over agency. This is not to deny individual voluntarism completely. When referring to social order that African traditional laws maintained, both Mbiti's (1969) and Tempels' (1959) above quotations refer to individuals, albeit as deviants to be punished if they failed to conform to the community binding rules. African traditional art is one area that can be used to make this point even more strongly.

At what point does the traditional African artist stop working on personal creative ideas and perfect his or her skills only to produce pieces of art that would embody communal values? Okpewho's (1977:309) analysis of the subject leads him to argue that:

> artists whose works enjoyed no patronage or adoption were doomed to oblivion, as their pieces crumbled with their homesteads. This situation has led art historians and critics to consider those pieces housed in a shrine or a palace, or else excavated in the vicinities of these, as the definitive output of the community, forgetting that much more that did not conform to the fashionable styles of the "schools" might have been done.

We can conclude from the above that individual Africans did have respect for traditional rules but they also made deliberate individual choices that would have helped or failed (been accepted or not by) the community. Likewise, the community would have set rules that helped or failed (were accepted or not by) the individuals. We cannot go back to pre-colonial times to prove the above point; we can, however, draw several examples from modern day Africa to highlight what is otherwise a 'winning and losing trust narrative' between structure and agency in Africa.

Trust: the go between

'Structure' winning and losing trust over 'agency'
It is hoped that the foregoing analysis of structure and agency has led to an understanding that both concepts have

analytical values. They refer to different ontological perspectives. Instead of being dismissive of each other, both structure and agency must be recognised and that any attempt to elevate one at the expense of the other would be futile. Proponents of an exclusive and impervious dualism between structure and agency must, however, recognise that the prospects of one (structure and agency) ontological perspective gaining prominence over another can be said to be on the basis of *trust and security* that structures represent for agents and vice versa.

Trust then is not a straightforward concept to understand. One of the key problems with *trust*, as stated towards the end of the first chapter, is our inability to penetrate human minds and confidently confirm their honest intentions. This *impossibility* is often replaced with *probability* or *improbability* of trustworthiness. Hence, trust is defined as the 'probability that he (structures or individuals to adapt 'he' to the argument here) will perform an action that is beneficial (...) is high enough for us to consider in engaging in some form of cooperation with him' (Gambetta 2000; Sapienza et al. 2013:1313). That probability is the result of a process (of leadership) at all levels (school, hospitals, media, government and especially politics) as a commentary in *Political Quarterly Publishing* (2004:99) states:

> It builds up slowly, but can dissipate rapidly under the impact of events (hence 'I will never trust you again'). It also functions as a kind of moral shorthand, avoiding the need for an elaborate moral judgemental calculus in our daily encounters with individuals, groups and institutions.

Africa is not the only place where trust seems to have eroded. In the UK, for example, the hacking and expenses scandals are two instances of trust being (having been) broken between structure and agency. The hacking scandal involved the News of the World Cooperation unlawfully and unethically accessing celebrities' and politicians' private voice messages. The expenses scandal lifted the lid on UK members of parliament's corrupt practice of fiddling with their expenses for personal financial gains at the cost of the taxpayer. These incidents have damaged that *moral shorthand* that is *trust* between institutions (structures) and members of the public or taxpayers, as is commonly used (agency).

While new and innovative ways of building trust are being thought about in various quarters, an existing policy divide on taxation and spending and the political rhetoric used to caricature rival parties epitomises my argument here. The conservative party, for example, strikes the agency cord by promising lower taxes and community based initiatives and in that way can be seen as trusting individuals to make the right decisions for their future. A small government then would relinquish 'state control' in favour of 'state steering' (Zambeta 2002). Without intending to do party politics, it can be argued that this is only part of the story. As already pointed out, individual actions can be egotistic, and investment in services of public interest (roads, hospitals, schools, energy, water systems, laws etc.,) requires not only further contributions but also a greater institutional involvement, which is the rhetoric of the labour party.

It is hard to articulate distinct political ideologies on the African continent but that is not to say that structure/agency and the issue of trust between them are inexistent. The era of political ideologies, as identified by Thomson (2004), is only a reality that emerged with the decolonisation of the African continent. African nationalism, socialism or other forms of ideology are said to have embodied values of unity, oneness and servitude leading to the banning of ethnic associations, other forms of political creeds. 'Nyerere, Senghor and Sékou Touré all stressed that there was a common ownership of the means of production (as all had access to land), while African leaders served rather than exploited their people' (Thomson 2004:85).

For Obiakor (2004:404), these are the patriotic leaders that Africa needs through 'the institutionalisation of a pragmatic system of African-centred education'. In Obiakor's world view, as indicated in the first chapter, this Afro-centric and patriotic leaders' discourse would represent a revival of pre-colonial or traditional African structures or systems and the values they represented. There is here an echo of consensus and shared decision making characteristic of collegial and participative models of leadership in the Western world (Bush 2011). This, however, must be understood in the context of existing hierarchically authoritarian forms of governance in various parts of Africa. The traditional African forms of structural organising may have had their successes and novelty in the values that they represented, but the purely altruistic leadership narrative could not be sustained in the face of what Thomson (2004) calls the crises of 'accumulation' and of 'governance', which led to the loss of 'the support of their citizens'.

There are several examples of agents (citizens) losing trust in structure (institutions) on the African continent, but two will suffice to illustrate the point.

The Unexpected Homecoming (Elonga Mboyo 2015) is the first example, in which I recount details of how I fell victim to Oscar Kopongo Kabata and his mafia-like family's dishonesty in honouring a tenancy agreement in the summer of 2014 in Kinshasa/DRC. Despite all the evidence I had pointing to either deliberate or *ad hoc* organised criminal activities, to everyone's amazement, when the concerned parties turned to the authorities to arbitrate, the justice system exonerated the very people who had straightforwardly breached the contract. It could be argued that this is not an isolated case in the DRC and/or other parts of Africa.

The Anglo-Leasing scandal in Kenya is another such example. Following the smooth political transition in Kenya from Moi to Kibaki's presidencies, the latter represented the hopes of the Kenyan masses for real political reforms. The new regime, Bachelard (2010) argues, brought some significant reforms in the area of education and showed early signs of real commitment to restore the rule of law and fight against corruption. However, with the Anglo-Leasing scandal, the Kenyan public and the rest of the world came to find out more about endemic corrupt practices that led to the award of a $35 million contract (and many more) to a bogus company that was not even registered in the UK.

Despite admissions by top ministers in Kibaki's government that they were involved in the scandal and that fees paid by the fake companies were intended to finance political campaigns, Githongo (the investigator) was advised by high ranking officials to drop his investigations and not to hand over his files of damning evidence to the Kenyan anti-corruption commission. Given the intense pressure that Githongo was under, he had to tender his resignation but published his report, which forced president Kibaki to sack and demote some of his ministers, only for them to be reinstated at a later date (Bachelard 2010:191-192).

One of Bachelard's concluding remarks is that domestic and international protests following the scandal 'contributed to the socialisation of the population into the norms of good governance' (2010:196). To echo the 'diminishing support of the citizens towards their institutions' theme from Thomson (2004), Bachelard argues that because the population is more socialised with the norms of good governance, their support or tolerance for corrupt regimes will be diminished.

The support element is what is referred to here as *trust* which, according to Thomson, can be regained through *constitutional mechanisms* that are put in place in certain liberal democracies. *Constitutional mechanisms* alone, it can be argued, have a static character to them and they can easily be ignored. The view here, therefore, is that such mechanisms need to be placed within a bigger picture of on-going social construction, which is exemplified through the duality of structures discussed in the latter part of this chapter.

'Agency' winning and losing trust over 'Structure'

In the interest of maintaining balance, the argument will now focus on identifying traces of trust narratives of human agency on the African continent. Not doing so would be perpetuating the same mistakes that Greenfield (1986:61) laments when he says:

We have a science of administration which can deal only with facts and which does so by eliminating from its consideration all human passion, weakness, conviction, hope, will, pity, frailty, altruism, courage, vice and virtue…in its own impotence, it is inward-looking, self-deluding, self-defeating, and unnecessarily boring.

In the context of African political systems, what Thomson (2004) calls a rejuvenated civil society could be used here as an example of the time of reckoning with human passion that Greenfield evokes. Thomson describes it with the following words:

Churches, trade unions, ethnic associations, women's organisations, professional bodies, farming co-operatives, community groups and eventually political parties, had all at some time played a key role in the fight against colonial rule. These same associational organisations would also contribute significantly to Africa's 'second liberation' of the late 1980s and early 1900s.

More recently, individual acts of discontent in North Africa that struck a chord with the general public and resulted in what is now commonly referred to as 'the Arab spring' can be viewed as the generalisation of what may have begun as isolated individual actions. The technological innovations in telecommunication in Kenya, individual philanthropic initiatives by the Multi-billionaire Mo Ibrahim and many others, illustrate Africa's agentic ability to effect positive change on the continent.

However, the above rather salvific and trust-inspiring agentic organising has not been replicated everywhere all the time. Letseke (2013), for example, gives a more up to date account of regrettable acts of indiscretions of human agency in South Africa. Echoing a theme of human agency and rational choice theory, Letseke identifies some of those indiscretions as in the form of violent crime, premeditated murder, rape, assault, homophobic attacks, police brutality and disregard for the rights of the minorities, such as pygmies and albinos, among other things.

One now needs to cast the mind back to the horrific killings that led to the loss of about 800,000 lives in Rwanda. On 6th April 1994, a missile hit the plane in which the then (Hutu) Rwandan president Habyarimana was travelling. His instant death triggered genocide by majority Hutus on minority Tutsis who were now blamed for the death of the president. Smeulers and Hoex (2010) represent the views of those who interpret this genocide as the failure of institutional structures with the following: 'violence almost immediately started in a very ordered and organised way, suggesting that the new power-holders had carefully prepared the genocide' (450-1). When attempting to capture the micro-perspective of the genocide, the authors carried out interviews in Rwanda that revealed 'social interaction among hands-on perpetrators and group dynamics provided better explanations of the genocide than widespread ethnic fear and hatred' (436). To illustrate the view that human agency, not just structure, has also let us down, Smeulers and Hoex's (2010) recount their Rwandan informants as saying the following:

'some of my friends became killers. What made them change was greed. To get something from the killings. Their main motivation was greed. (Prisoner Y). 'It felt secure in the group and that was a reason to join (Prisoner W) (444).

Smeulers and Hoex's (2010) perspective is not entirely new. In 2008, the Rwandan academic Jean-Paul Kimonyo had published 'Un Génocide Populaire', in which he demonstrated a greater involvement of human agency. To reiterate once more, the view that Kimonyo (2008) advances is that, while the horrific actions that resulted in genocide in Rwanda had received institutional/structural blessing or backing, there was evidence, even in the predominantly Tutsi populated areas, to suggest that there were social interactional motives that guided the atrocities that led to people killing their neighbours.

Things may have changed now, but back in the 1990s it was the Kenyan government's policy that any citizen from West Africa, especially those from Cameroon and Nigeria, could not enter into Kenya except through Nairobi international airport. My Cameroonian friends who once travelled over land from Kampala to the Kenyan border were sent back. With valid visas, their only option was to fly into Nairobi. The reason for that, we were told, stemmed from previous individual acts by some West Africans in dealing drugs, which made the Kenyan institutions lose trust and make Nairobi's international airport the only entry point, where they could, using modern equipment, effectively screen these 'dubious' subjects. Trust towards human agency here becomes a rare commodity.

Attempts to curtail such vice and broken trust on the part of human agency can lead to the prevalence of institutional or structural attempts to control and prevent any further mishaps. This can sometimes take the form of developmental projects (Arthur 1991) conceived with the intent of influencing institutional policy. There may have been improvements in how much government policies are founded or rooted in empirical referents (Howlett and Weelstead 2011) in other parts of the world. In Africa, however, such empirical referents or a *real* agentic involvement is compromised by lack of transparency, corruption, clientelism, mismanagement of public funds and lack of separation between the ruling party/leaders and the state, an unfortunate side of a one party system that emerged with the intention of maintaining unity following independence (Thomson 2004).

37

Crisis of trust?

It will not be the first time that the phrase 'crisis of trust' is used. O'Neil (2002) voiced questions about trust in relation to the accountability culture and the 'audit explosion' in the UK. With the foregoing discussion in mind, it is legitimate to argue that the leadership crisis in Africa has been about 'a crisis of trust' between structure and agency with each presenting an unconvincing trust narrative. Mending such a 'crisis of trust' may depend on the choices of those people concerned in a particular social context. In most cases, the first initiatives have come from institutions or structures. After all, they are the ones that control various resources. Some initiatives (for example the audit culture in the UK) may be perceived as impinging on professional autonomy, but *'if they work'* in terms of transparency in the running of public affairs, it may not matter to some that 'targets, outcome-based evaluation, and bureaucratic form-filling in every professional arena has shifted the basis of professional work, trust and accountability' (Lunt 2008:85).

In the light of the argument presented here so far, one needs to take a position with regard to how trust between structure and agency, especially in Africa, can be rebuilt. The position here, therefore, is that *'what works'* should not be imposed by institutions on agents, but any resolution for a course of action that is the result of structure/agency interactions. This is consistent with Giddens' duality of structures within his structuration theory needing further elaboration.

Duality of structures:

For Giddens (1974:5), social reality is a recursive reproduction of social practices where 'structure is both medium and outcome'. One of Giddens' concerns, which is discussed more extensively in the methodology section, was the relegation of agents as knowing actors in a society or structures of which they are members. Aware of the unconscious and tacit stocks of

38

knowledge side of human experience, actors are constantly involved in the 'discursive consciousness' and 'have some degree of discursive penetration of the social systems to whose constitution they contribute' (5). Stones (2005) argues, and it is also the view here, that because of the structure/agency interaction in the reproduction of social life, both structure-and-agency are present in the constitution of structure as medium and outcome. The constitution of social life, therefore, is not done by structure *on behalf of* agents or vice versa but as *a joint effort*. The same thing can arguably be said about leadership and just about anything, including democracy.

Speaking about the spread of democracy around the world, Giddens (2002) notes what he terms the 'paradox of democracy'. What he means is that, while new democracies continue to emerge, suggesting the popularity of the concept and its practices, there is disillusionment taking over the old ones (meaning Western democracies), which is symptomatic of the crisis of trust. To overcome this 'paradox of democracy', Giddens suggests the 'democratisation of democracies'. By this he means: making democracies more democratic.

One criticism that can be made of Giddens is his suggestion that the West is the epicentre of democracy, a topic that is discussed more extensively in Chapter 4. Ayittey (2010:1184) refutes such suggestions and argues that 'just because there were no ballot boxes in African villages does not mean African natives had no understanding of the essence of democracy'. From Ayittey's perspective, duality of structures would be an African concept for Africans to own and hold on to. But from various accounts (Bachelard 2010; Thomson 2004; and many more), it is obvious that government institutions have made a 90-degree turn away (unscientific sampling) from whatever essence of democracy Africa may have had. An articulation of those very African concepts (democracy, and structuration theory in this case) is therefore necessary.

To return to the idea of 'democratisation of democracies', its parallel in Giddens' conceptualisation of duality of structures would read like: 'dualitisation of duality of structures'. While the ideas of democracy and 'duality of structures' have to be conceived of in a relative way, they are not a given in all contexts. Their existence is disputed and contested in some places more than in others.

Hence, the very idea of *democratising democracies* or *dualitising duality of structures* begs the question whether such a reality already exists and only needs evolving and developing. There are no easy answers or positions one can take without being labelled as either defending the cause of the elites, who control structures by denying the people the opportunity to shape and reshape their structures, or being seen as a neo-colonial mouthpiece, detached from reality and failing to recognise local efforts by local leaders to bring about duality of structures.

Given the broken trust within various fields, in the way that has been argued here, the discursive joint actions of reproduction are what is proposed as the way forward in which both structure and agency's broken trust narratives, especially on the African continent, can be restored. This sort of argument may be seen as a mere responsibility sharing and tension breaking strategy, just in case joint structure and agency constitution of social life turns out not to embody and incarnate a people's aspirations. If we go it alone, what if things do not turn out as we expect them to? The 'what if' approach is a weak premise on which to base the duality of structures and restore trust. It is self-centred because it has personal interests to think about in case things did not work.

The then Zaire case study adapted from Thomson (2004) illustrates to a certain degree some disingenuous ways to build partnerships to make them appear like genuine duality of structures. After systematically plundering the wealth meant for his compatriots, Mobutu (the then president of Zaire) witnessed a period where his citizens disengaged with his many governments, foreign powers disowned him and outside investors became reluctant to do any business with a bunch of corrupt officials. Thomson describes the final months or years of Mobutu's 32 year regime in the following words:

Mobutu attempted to cling to power, despite the growing strength of opposition groups. Forced to liberalise the constitution, he still managed to stall his opponents with a series of political manoeuvres, including constitutional conventions, the postponement of multi-party elections, the funding of numerous bogus opposition parties, and by simply buying off opposition leaders. In the end, the country was left in constitutional deadlock, just as it had been at the start of Mobutu's 32-year reign. The president refused to relinquish control of what remained of the executive and the army, while opposition leaders in parliament failed to command the political strength to remove him (224).

The reading of the above extract is slightly different here. The contention here is that the Mobutu regime had been heavily reliant on structuralism. What counted was the will of the president through the institutions. Aware of his imminent downfall and worried about losing his grip on power, he began to ease the tensions and project an image of social reality that is shaped and reshaped by all agents of the country's society. Since it was started on a weak premise (that of retaining power for oneself), it had to resort to all sorts of malpractices (creation of bogus parties, promising and postponing constitutional conventions etc.). Any apparent cohesion was the result of agents being 'drawn into a process as ambiguous beings…they merely imagine they have reached power' (Freire 1996:108).

A strong trust restoring duality of structures is a form of coalition or partnership in the sense of 'an organisation of diverse interest groups that combine their human and material resources to effect a specific change the members are unable to bring about independently' (Brown 1984). It emancipates, educates, plans, adapts and takes responsibility. Whether we refer to them as advocacy, progressive alliances, or collaborations, the sort of partnership that is being advocated for here, through duality of structures, has an echo of Mizrahi

41

and Rosenthal's (2001) conceptual framework for successful coalitions. The authors identify *conditions, commitment, contributions* and *competence*.

1. Among the *conditions*, the authors identify: political and economic realities; resources available within organisations; community climate and past experiences with alliances... and arguably the experiences of trust that both structure and agency have projected.

2. *Commitment* is more about the ideology that is based on public interest rather than personal gains in resources and power.

3. In terms of *contributions*, those could be understood to be the identification of both tangible and intangible resources that structure and agency bring to the table, their ideologies that need the investment of time and energy and the power to engage in action that would lead to specific goals.

4. On the level of *competence*, the authors argue for the analytical and interactional skills needed to achieve goals, maintain internal relations and, more importantly for the argument here, 'developing trust with, accountability to, and contributions from, the coalition membership base (Rosenthal and Mizrahi 1994)'. (Mizrahi and Rosenthal 2001:55-65).

It is necessary at this stage to develop and link the above concepts with the argument being made in this chapter. What it is not doing is advocating for coalition governments or governance of whichever institutions, in the sense that rival parties must be included in all structures, but that such structures must reflect the partnership between structure and agency. As it is more explicitly articulated in the fourth aspect of the above conceptual framework, the unfolding of the social reality that meets that criterion is what Echterhoff et al. (2009) call shared reality. In circumstances where there is not much commitment to duality of structures, and if anyone cared at all, the general population will be told what the structure, as outcome, is projected to be or has been, without involving them in the shaping or process of it.

The above authors stress the importance of process for achieving outcomes that would be part of a shared reality. In their analysis of the different dimensions in which reality can be said to be shared, they insist that 'communication highlights a potentially important everyday mechanism underlying the construction of culturally shared memories and evaluation of the world - a basic mechanism for constructing social, cultural and political beliefs' (Echterhoff et al. 2009:515). Those involved in that construction (structure and agency), they argue, need to do the following: 'rather than remembering or evaluating the topic information as originally given, the communicator will remember or evaluate the information as represented after taking the viewpoint of the audience into account' (*ibid*). To effectively do this in a continent like Africa that is still entrenched in high levels of intimidation and autocratic rule, structure needs to demonstrate an *increasing sense of self-scrutiny* that should lead to a *decreasing sense of fear* in the population (agents) and encourage them to engage with the shaping of their social reality. This emerging idea has already been advanced in the first chapter and is the methodology of structuration that I unpack in Chapter 7.

Conclusion

The influential work of Paolo Freire in *Pedagogy of the Oppressed* (1970) might be a fitting way to conclude this chapter. The distinction that the author makes between oppressed and oppressors in this master piece can be compared to agency and structure dualism. While the oppressed are portrayed by the author as victims of oppression and only cautioned to avoid dehumanising themselves by oppressing their former oppressors, the view in this chapter is that neither structure nor agency can claim the moral high ground, given their respective failures as discussed earlier. We have a tendency to pick the

43

lesser of two evils. The difference in this case, especially in the African context, is that those who control power and the means of production in these sovereign nations have no independent third party to decide which is the lesser evil between: structures that they (the elites) have become inseparable from and the larger population ('agents' for Giddens or 'the oppressed' to use Freire's term).

Embracing duality of structures could mean giving up on hard fought freedom from colonial oppression and this may explain the intransigence of both the remnants of independence fighters and newly elected leaders on the African continent who characterise Western critical views on their regimes as neo-colonialism. In such a situation, and given all the state's resources under their control, structures are likely to self-appoint as the lesser of the two evils (between structure and agency). The imbalance of power, therefore, works in favour of structures (or the elites), whose media machines will claim that the social, political and economic reality they are defending is a shared reality between structure and agency. Such propaganda may be directed at outsiders whose interventions could be viewed as interference but it does not automatically restore the broken trust between structure and agency of a given setting (or nation).

Restoring that trust, as argued here, would require the application of the duality of structures. To borrow from Freire (1970), structure and agency would have to engage in a dialogical theory of action, where communication is not the 'depositing of communiques whose contents are intended to exercise a domesticating influence' (112) but instead be based on true commitment to transforming action, which 'cannot fail to assign the people a fundamental role in the transformation process' (107). Assigning others a role is as important as assigning oneself a role that effectively invites others to take up theirs. That can be realised with increasing self-scrutiny on the part of structures (or the leaders and the elites who are their mouthpieces) and decreasing fear on the part of the agents (actors or, in other words, the larger population). The idea of STRUGGLE comes to mind here as an essential concept when thinking about African ontological identity(ies). Given its fluidity, I interrogate the concept of 'struggle' in the next chapter.

Chapter 3

Duality of structures: a (not THE) methodology

Abstract

The argument in the previous chapter came down to identifying *trust* as a key element if structure were to win the upper hand over agency, and vice versa. With examples of a tumultuous relationship of broken promises, it was suggested that rather than bemoan the conflation that structuration theory brings about, it could instead be deemed beneficial to look at the value of mixing structure and agency in restoring lost trust, especially in different fields (politics, schools, hospitals, police, etc.) across the African continent. In the first chapter, it was argued that *increasing self-scrutiny* on the part of leaders, representing structures, *and decreasing fear* on the part of citizens of African nations, representing agency, were the measures of the struggle for a healthier partnership between structure and agency, in the light of Giddens' structuration theory. Based on those indicators, this chapter develops the thinking a bit further by seeking to identify where they sit within the ontological and methodological issues that might be encountered.

Introduction

This chapter discusses the ontological and methodological issues that could be associated with restoring *trust* in structure and agency social interactions across the fields of politics, educational, health etc. on the African continent. Having become familiar with Antony Giddens' structuration theory from reading the previous chapters, there might not be anything novel in the ontological argument. However, the methodological discussion takes the reader into new territory.

The chapter begins with parallel ontological, as well as epistemological, discussions that are consistent with structuration theory and the African worldview. Upon closer scrutiny, I argue for an ontological unity between structuration theory and African ontology (ntu). This is followed by a discussion of the methodological logic of enquiry and a brief overview of possible strategies that could be adopted when researching a topic with elements of duality of structures. Given the tumultuous and contested political and cultural environment on the African continent, which seems to affect the way business is run in other fields, this chapter explores some pertinent ethical issues, which could be minimised or avoided through a better understanding and application of duality of structures. The chapter ends with the introduction of (critical) discourse analysis as a viable option for data analysis.

Ontology

Grix (2002:177) argues that 'ontology is the starting point of all research, after which one's epistemological and methodological positions logically follow'. Like Grix, Blaikie (2000:8) regards ontological assumptions as 'concerned with what we believe constitutes social reality'. Giddens was dissatisfied with extreme dualism between objectivism/structuralism and subjectism/constructivism. As ontological alternatives, objectivism or structuralism represents 'an ontological position that asserts that social phenomena and their meanings have an existence that is independent of social actors'.Subjectism/constructivism with agency 'is an alternative ontological position asserting that social phenomena and their meanings are continually being accomplished by social actors' (Grix 2002).

Stones (2005) distinguishes between 'ontology in general' and 'ontology *in-situ*'. The former refers to the abstract and the philosophical while the latter describes the substantive and empirical concept. His understanding of Giddens' ontology embedded in the theory of structuration reads like this:

He (meaning Giddens) developed his notions of them (meaning structure and agency) in abstract terms so that the conceptual definitions he settled for would encompass all structures and all agents, the very nature of time and space. In other words, he wanted to capture the general characteristics of these entities so that the concepts would be useful to the widest possible set of circumstances across times and spaces (7).

With that characterisation of Giddens' ontological argument, Rob Stones hopes to advance what he terms '*strong structuration*', which is based on concrete empirical entities, ontology-*in-situ*. The position here is that, while discussions about ontological assumptions may start off being abstract, they remain assumptions, which are impossible to refute empirically as Hughes and Sharrock (1997, pp. 5–6) contend. Giddens may have given ontological 'ideal types' (to use a Weberian phrase) of structure and agency that would be useful for the widest possible set of circumstances across times and spaces but, using Hughes and Sharrock's assertion, these assumptions have a situational existence that is impossible to refute.

With the above discussion in mind, it could be argued, therefore, that the 'trans-situational' can only stand on the basis of real situational properties. Hence, *ontology-in-situ* is effectively built into *ontology-in-general*. Keeping the two together is not only consistent with Giddens' ontological argument, but also serves as a powerful tool to understand, as well as overcome, some of the ethical problems that one could encounter when engaged in researching the African social phenomenon from this ontological mind-set.

The differentiation in terms of *ontology-in-general* and *ontology-in-situ*, one might argue, is more of a technical exercise rather than pointing to a starkly different version of ontological reality. Besides, Giddens, like any other before him, thought of structure and agency as pointing to real entities in the conventional sense, which could be represented by entities such as family, government and schools on the one hand and individual acts on the other hand. His *duality of structures'* characterisation of social phenomenon can then be thought of, as Stones (2005:6) rightly does, as 'focused directly on the processes and practices involved at the point of interaction' between the conventional entities of structures and agencies. Research based on duality of structures, therefore, transcends this clear cut ontological position and sees reality as neither nor but instead based on both.

Now, where do previous conceptualisations about African ontology(ies) fit into the above discussion about duality of structures? Are they so far apart that it would render their apparent amalgamation far-fetched? While Africa cannot be denied its uniqueness and idiosyncrasies, denying that there can never be points of (ontological) commonality with the rest of the world begs the question why we have African, Trans-Atlantic, transnational black ontologies in the first place, given the multiplicity of African contexts. That would only strengthen the biased proposition that one hybridised discourse, in the form of a collective African ontology (Puri 2004), often seen through profound cultural unity (Anta Diop 1962) and sometimes imaged as 'one cultural river' (Molefi and Kariamu Asante 1990), is more appealing than another hybridised discourse (seeing a convergence between African ontology and an ontology based on structuration theory). The proponents of a clear cut ontological divide need to bear in mind the fact that 'the terms "Western" and "non-Western" (*structuration theory and African ontology in this case* - my italics) may (and often do) reflect biased and loaded assumptions' (Reagan 2005:11). Instead of co-opting the clear cut Western versus African ontological assumptions, it is the view here that an ontological commonality/unity is demonstrable even if one has started from the African ontological perspective – ntu.

African ontology is a minefield and we are nowhere near reaching a consensus on African worldview, whether opposed or similar to the Western worldview. It is also worth stating that some of the work having contributed to an entrenched division in perceptions of worldviews (ontologically, epistemologically, axiologically and methodologically) has, according to Dixon (1977:121), failed to articulate or account for 'the origin, historical development, or the generic bases of the two worldviews'. Here, I will attempt to provide a generic ontological point of convergence between African ontology and the theory of structuration.

Focusing on the African worldview, the discourse seems somewhat territorial with the African continent and its intellectuals 'who never made the crossing' into North America being seen as playing a peripheral role in the construction of African identity (Bhambra et al. 2014:294). This mutating field has prompted others to look beyond the *trans-Atlantic* slave trade and propose the *transnational* views of African thoughts, in order to open the discussions to other experiences of collective black identity (Wright 2010). There are Africans who are not black and even blacks who are not Africans. I use Africa and black interchangeably to ensure that no one feels left out.

That said, African ontology or ontologies can be understood as a way of 'acknowledging Africa and the traditions of African thought' (Bhambra et al. 2014) and I will add 'body to reflect the totality of an African (see more on Body sociology and Africa in Chapter 6). If we look at structuration theory as an entirely western thought, African ontology would be about understanding social reality from an entirely African perspective. Only, as I see it here, such an entirely African perspective is not far from structuration theory.

Let us assume that the 'authentic' African thought/identity has been obscured for several historical reasons. Those reasons may be about the Apartheid in South Africa, colonialism across the whole continent, segregation and racism that the black collective have and continue to endure and all their consequential impacts on other social interactions. The non-territorial approach would be to see, in the above experiences, some commonality among those of African descent who crossed the Atlantic to America, those who remained on the continent and even those who, through other trajectories, constitute the African diaspora today. The common denominator for all these experiences can be put under the umbrella of supremacy and dominance. It is (white) supremacy or dominance that stands in the way of (obscures) African ontological identity. The struggle AGAINST that domination is what has been at the forefront of the liberation narrative.

Before we provide a response and prove how this relates to structuration theory, it is important to peddle back to the proposition that the sought after African identity is obscured. In some quarters, the emancipatory birthing of an African ontology is already a reality, albeit 'à priori'. Carroll (2014) makes the point that an African view of ontology is essentially spiritual, as opposed to the European one which is material. As a result, European Epistemology relies on the five senses while, for Africans, knowledge can be acquired in ways other than through senses - spiritually. Carrol, however, concludes, rightly or wrongly, 'that due to the inability...to ground ...work within a culturally-specific conceptual framework...a Black Sociology has never truly occurred' (ibid 260). It is not the mission here to enter into a defence mode of Myers' (1987) work on which Carroll's (2014) argument is based. What must be acknowledged, however, is the fact that this is a contested field planted against the backdrop of STRUGGLE AGAINST domination and supremacy.

Without repeating the argument in Chapters 1 & 2 and further illustrated by the forgoing discussion, the ontological thinking here departs from the idea of struggle (between structure and agency) and, on that basis alone, the argument that this publication advances is rooted within the very essence of

African reality. The decolonising process, leading to the excavation of an authentic pre-domination/colonial African identity, may not be elusive and futile if it is built on identifying the historical manifestations of the struggle between structure and agency. It is a struggle that is so that one cannot step on the same river twice. Africa and Africans are not robotically static but rather dynamic agents capable of making conventions around values that they press into perpetuity.

I want to move beyond a selective and narrow understanding of struggle aimed singularly at a fixed oppressor (racist institution, individuals or colonisers 'of yesterday?'). The struggle must be thought more broadly first and foremost as one against oppression and dominance of any shape and form, whether it has an Eastern, Northern, Southern, Western and even African label on it. In the wake of nation states, much of the struggle was AGAINST a moveable or displaceable occupier who the freedom fighters wanted to leave and return to their countries (Europe). We live in a world where even the 'oppressed' has also packed his bags and gone to live in the 'oppressor's' heartland (diasporan communities), or oppression has been camouflaged in some forms of modernity (Bhambra et al. 2014), through international and regional bodies.

Worse still, African nationalist institutions, which unlike the colonisers cannot be subjected to the same fate of being forced to return to a geographical space (Europe) they set out from, have become predatory bodies. As it was illustrated in the second chapter, African agents have also faltered too, leading to the loss of trust. In this scenario, the suggestion here, in line with structuration theory is to look at struggle not as AGAISNT either structure or agency, but as struggle FOR cooperation between structure and agency. The African ontology, therefore, cannot be divorced from the idea of struggle for cooperation.

Another way of conceptualising struggle for cooperation is by using the terms 'force' or 'force-beings'. 'The ontology of the Bantu relates to the key root *ntu*, and signifies force' (Smart 2008). Without seeking to (re)calibrate what has been said about

Ubuntu and other concepts with the *ntu* root, when Archbishop Desmond Tutu (2010:23) says 'in Africa, recognition of our interdependence is called Ubuntu', one cannot possibly limit that interdependence to only between individuals (agents) where it is understood solely as 'a person depends on others just as much as others depend on him/her' (Letseka 200:184). Such a view fails to grasp the full meaning of 'force being' (*ntu*) which has both spiritual and social realms.

The spiritual realm brings God into the equation. There has been a divide between those who conceive of a creator God as either the ultimate force-being or of a nature far greater than and different from worldly force-beings (Smart 2008). On the basis of the argument suggested in this publication, I take the view that God for Africans is and should be a being of a nature far greater than and different from force-beings of the universe. To say that God is the ultimate force-being is to suggest that s/he is the resolution, the point of harmony or unifying point of the other two force-beings: what I call the primary force-beings (humans) and the secondary force-beings (institutions which are the creation of the primary force-beings). God then is the perfection of all force-beings.

There is an attractive side to that sort of theology, since it infuses Africans with the hope that they will one day be like God. The negative side of that is it postpones (pushes back) the complete harmony between structure and agency force-beings until the eschaton (the end of the world as a final divine event). Structuration theory then becomes one of Weberian ideal types, which for Giddens (2001:14) are 'analytical models that can be used to understand the world. In the real world, ideal types rarely, if ever, exist – often only some of their attributes will be present'. Ubuntu or structuration theory, as presented here, is not an ideal type on the basis that only agents are first degree force-being. They are 'created directly by God'. Structures (institutions), on the other hand, are second degree force-beings in that they are the creation of agents (of the first degree force-beings).

In the social realm then, you have the primary force-beings (individuals) and secondary force-beings (African institutions) where, as well as living out the maxim of "'a person is a person through other persons', the idea of Ubuntu envisages individuals and community living as a relational entity, each giving value, purpose and identity to the other" (Littrel et al. 2013:235). I take the view that God did not create communities of Africans (African governments, African Union, globalisation through institutions such as the United Nations, World bank... for that matter) but s/he created Africans (primary first beings), who organised themselves into communities (secondary force beings) and carved themselves an Ubuntu (structuration theory) worldview of recursive-ness and interdependence between force beings (structure and agency).

In view of the above discussion, a number of deductions can be made at this point: 1) that sociologically speaking, Ubuntu signifies interdependence between individuals as well as individuals (primary force-beings) and structures (secondary force-beings); 2) Structure and agency can be viewed as primary and secondary force-beings not fighting AGAINST each other but intertwined in cooperation for a better future; and 3) that the very essence of such an interdependence resides in the reconciliation between agents and their own creation (structure) here and now. The figure below captures the foregoing discussion and demonstrates how the title of this book could read *Africa through Ubuntu: The FS (fear and self-scrutiny) methodology of Structuration.*

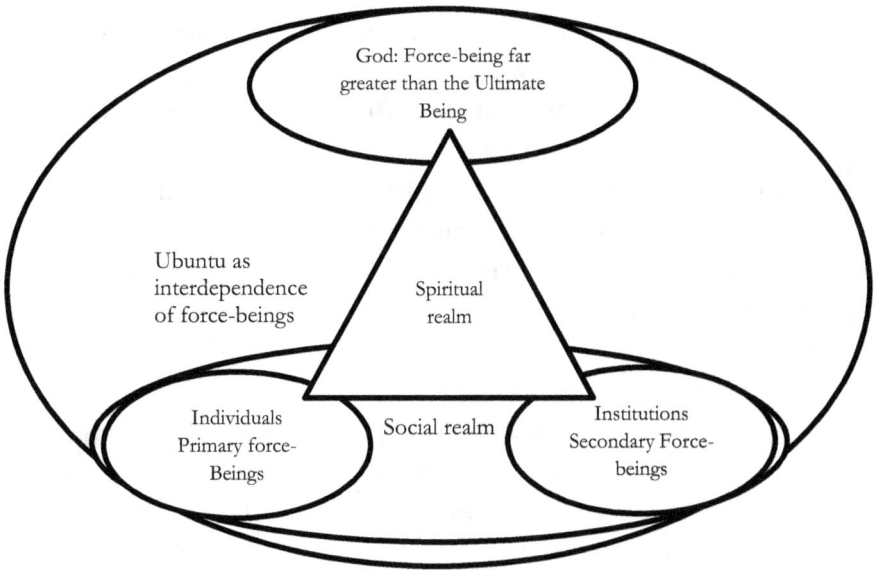

Diagram showing an oval containing a triangle. The triangle is labelled at its top vertex "God: Force-being far greater than the Ultimate Being" and inside "Spiritual realm". To the left: "Ubuntu as interdependence of force-beings". At the bottom are three inner ovals: "Individuals Primary force-Beings", "Social realm", and "Institutions Secondary Force-beings".

If this *ntu* concept belonging to African traditional philosophy can be used to shape future ontology and the understanding of African social phenomena, then we can perhaps conceive of an African ontology that, through interdependent force-beings, is able to look back in order to look forward. It therefore allows me to tentatively refute Gyekye's (1995) call for a separation between traditional and modern African philosophy and join a chorus of other Africanists who believe that 'our traditions are modern, our modernities are traditional' (Leonardi 2004:661).

The continuity from traditional to modern African philosophy must not be mistaken to mean the replacement of African structures, as defined by institutions themselves, in place of European ones. This Hegelian style is what is wrong with Obiakor's approach, which does not articulate how our structures are to be formed and therefore leaves the door open for the exclusion of agency. Our traditions will truly be modern

56

only when modern African life is the result of a continuous intersection/interdependence between structure and agency (duality of structures) -*ntu*. We can express 'structure and agency ntu ontology' differently by means of Weibust's (1989) analytical tool for understanding traditions. That is to say that even though we may not be able to excavate the historical (African) traditions, as in the content of what took place in the pre-colonial era, the *ntu* ontology of interdependence between structure and agency force-beings provides Africans with a mechanism to interpret traditions (in defining what they believe to have taken place historically) and/or remain open to, as well as seek to understand, contemporary traditions (the way in which interpreted traditions and other factors such as moderation, the need for skilled work force and increasing demand for value society, is manifested in people's lives today). Rather than simply stating that duality of structures is the basis of one's ontological study, a discussion on how that translates into an epistemology and methodology in a given context is necessary.

Epistemology

While the recursive-ness of social reality in the duality of structures (of force-beings) may be an ongoing and stable process, what is reproduced is changeable unless structure and agency elect to place certain aspects of their interactions beyond their constant interplay. Some provisions in national constitutions in most African nations have this stable and 'objective' nature. Such rules that, according to Giddens (1979), enable and facilitate desired actions, may project the nature of reality and the knowledge to be derived from it as a fixed entity. Structuralism is clearly embedded in the duality of structures. The temptation, therefore, is to seek to know structure which is both medium and outcome in a positivistic way, meaning scientifically verified and proven. The positivistic charge is, in fact, what Africanists level against European epistemologies, which rely on the five senses (Carroll 2014). In the context of ontology of 'struggle FOR cooperation' between structure and agency (primary and secondary force-beings), the positivistic view needs to be tempered with the understanding of ontology-in-general being infused with ontology-in-situ. That means questioning and revising the doxa that Africans' knowledge base is only configured subjectively in a telepathic and spiritual realm (Carroll 2014). By bringing structure and agency together, one can argue that this is only possible within the framework of an epistemic interdependence between the two.

Stones (2007) acknowledges that 'few assume today that there is a simplistic linear step-by-step model of the research process; one can tinker with each step if necessary to conduct enquiry' (271). Therefore, the thinking that if one starts from a structuralist ontology, he or she will end up choosing a positivistic epistemological approach. The same goes for subjective ontology for interpretivist epistemologies, which is problematic when faced with an ontological position that starts with recognition of interplay between structure and agency. It can be argued that the fact that one starts research from an interpretivist epistemological standpoint does not negate the duality of structures, which, as already mentioned, does not preclude the 'trans-situational' and the 'situational'. The challenge for researchers then is to devise a methodology that recognises the interdependence of both structure and agency (of primary and secondary force-beings). The next section attempts to do just that.

Methodology

'Methodology is concerned with the logic of scientific inquiry; in particular with investigating the potentialities and limitations of particular techniques or procedures' (Grix 2002:179). The main question, Grix goes on to say is 'how do we go about enquiring about knowledge?' (180). To answer this question one needs to explicitly show an interest in both structure and agency if one is to remain committed to a study based on duality of structures with an ontological interplay.

It was demonstrated in Chapter 2 that in a world of clear cut ontological perspectives based on the structure and agency dualism, both structure and agency have sought to persuade or force each other to recognise their trustworthiness. Rebuilding that broken trust means that for both structure and agency's actions to be configured as 'joint actions', they have to overlap consensually. To overlap in the sense that the very essence of structure and agency's actions is the power those actions have in inciting and inviting the other to recreate the social phenomenon within the boundaries of decency and civility. The decency and civility environment could also be conceived of as having respect to the rule of ethical laws and upholding basic human rights. It is only in this context that one can envisage the appropriate sequence of duality of structures interaction. In 'post-conflict' and/or 'post-dictatorship' Africa, it is possible to envisage a nation seriously committed to the path of rebuilding trust and fostering ethically sound ways for advancing the economic prospects of its people, to witness moments where actors' *fearless* (intellectual or emotional) posture to engage with their structures is met, not with an iron fist, but with genuine and *increasing acts of self-scrutiny* on the part of the leaders who represent official institutions/structures. That, however, is not always the case, as I demonstrate in Chapter 7 where I outline the methodology of structuration. Whatever the change (positive or negative) resulting from this interplay is effectively structure as medium and outcome.

It was argued in previous chapters that the ups and downs of African leadership were the result of the neglect or consideration of human agency, in what should be the interplay of structure and agency in the formation of social reality. Given the history of power imbalance, where state machinery has been used to suppress individual agency, some African scholars have suggested different methodological approaches. One example will suffice to illustrate the difference with what I am proposing here.

The concept of Black radicals to manifest a tradition of resistance is taking hold in North American Africana literature. The idea highlights the audacity to speak the truth to dominating powers and consolidate a disparaging black identity (Quan and Willoughby-Herard 2013). What is crucial here is the above authors' claim that speaking the truth to dominating powers 'offers a methodological resistance to the insularity and despair of some forms of nationalism while simultaneously attending to the crisis of the Black petite-bourgeois about their almost systematic compromises with whomever appeared to be the ruling class' (ibid 111).

It is the belief here that the two indicators for duality of structures discussed in this publication offer a two-pronged methodological approach, which grounds the above claim. While we accept that speaking the truth is the right thing to do, one can only do that from a methodological position of *decreasing fear* from agents. *Decreasing fear*, in turn, can flourish (though not exclusively) if structure is *increasingly self-scrutinising* or vice versa. These two methodological dispositions can be taken up as viable research projects. Let us take the example of the impact that the diaspora has on its homeland. It is perhaps the case that in an age of the internet, the diaspora's opinions will somewhat weigh on internal politics of some countries. What is well documented, however, is that direct tax payment to an African government, in the case of Eritreans living abroad or hometown associations where help is directly channelled to family or town members back in countries of origin (Newland and Patrick 2004), can uplift the economics of a country. What a researching Africanist can do, therefore, is to assess the degree to which those diasporan interventions palliate the situation, make agents indifferent and tame their fearlessness on the one hand and implicitly justify, connive with or endorse some self-defending instead of self-scrutinising structures.

There is, however, another way of assessing *increasing self-scrutiny* and *decreasing fear*. There is a common sense view that if you want to know how people feel about something, you only have to ask them; or if you want to see how they live out their ideals then you only have to observe or study the trails of their lives through art, songs, and documents. This gives some insights as to the type of research that may be carried out. For example, there might be studies based on people's narratives, case studies, and phenomenological experiences that assess the above two indicators. Interviews, focus group studies, observations, artistic and text-based analyses can be envisaged in order to collect data.

There is a plethora of literature on qualitative research methods and it is outside the scope of this chapter to discuss the ins and outs of what is involved in choosing this or that method in qualitative research. However, Marshall and Rossman (2011), for example, can be a useful starting point for a comprehensive guide to issues in that regard. Instead, the focus here will turn to the seven categories that Marshall and Rossman use to underpin their discussions about qualitative research methods. The categories are particularly useful here when thinking about and preparing to overcome potential ethical issues of prime importance when carrying out a duality of structures inspired research in most countries on the African continent. Those categories invite a researcher to ask the following questions: what is the nature of the research? What is the relationship with participants? What is the direction of gaze? What is the purpose of the research? Who is the intended audience? What is the researcher political position? And what are the researcher's views on agency?

The African experience of agency still has some way to go before we can hope for not only the realisation of an authentic African ontology through the struggle for cooperation between structure and agency but also the production of knowledge in various fields. An agent (journalist and researcher for example), who is in a *decreased fear* mode, would not only be encouraged to

61

feel free to report and research the African reality but also be supported with the necessary resources and space. The unstable political environment in Africa, which I interpret to also imply lack of self-scrutiny, continues to restrict academic freedom and jeopardise the prospects of independent inquiry for the production of much needed knowledge for development (Benneh 2002).

The aforementioned questions certainly deserve a thorough examination by anyone considering engaging in a study that is based on duality of structures, even if the researcher's answers to the above questions coincide with the views of those whose social phenomenon is the subject of inquiry. Finding answers to those questions becomes even more imperative when the subjects of a given study do not share the views of the researcher. In such a scenario, the researcher would be faced with thorny ethical issues that he or she has to resolve. The next section will discuss some specific ethical issues of relevance relating to worldview, power, ontology-in-situ, catch and context in Africa.

Ethical issues and dilemmas

Worldview: The biggest problem in proposing an enquiry based on people's experiences is the degree to which their accounts are perceived to represent reality. Some of us want objectivity in what we claim and, more often than not, we want convincing evidence that is devoid of any subjective perceptions, which are subject to time, space, moods, ethnic and religious affiliations etc. Ontologically speaking, such an approach would view institutions (schools, hospitals, and all the cross-fields) as outside the realm of individuals and subjective perceptions. Another worldview might favour the views of individuals at the expense of reality as defined by structure. A third approach that is being proposed here brings structure and agency, objective and subjective,onto the same level playing field. Determining the nature of the research as being based on duality of structures (not to say ...*ntu*, 'struggle for cooperation' ontology) and sharing it with people who are not only the subjects of the study but also subjects who do not necessarily share the researcher's worldview, can lead to *clashing worldviews, permission and access issues* that must be anticipated.

Reiterating the importance of worldview, Carroll (2014:263) argues that 'it is incumbent upon African-centred sociologists and social theorists to develop theories, concepts and models and produce research that is within the cultural parameters reflective of African descended people'. This publication responds to that by offering analytical framework(s) for researching and understanding African social phenomena. Carroll's point, however, is also an indictment of the African scholar who has spent most of his/her time and energy fighting a fixed oppressor (colonisers and neo-colonisers) and by default absolved the nationalist oppressor/trust breaker (either structure or agency, see Chapter 2) instead of elaborating a worldview (based on various force-beings) towards oppression and transgression of any kind. An anecdotal and perhaps trivial example, but nevertheless illustrative of the absolution reserved to nationalists but not to 'fixed' oppressors and those who have come to represent them, is in the use of the 'derogatory' term *nigger*: a reference we black people are allowed, absolved to use on ourselves but would take offence to it coming from a white person.

Power: In social systems with *unequal balance of power* reflected through authoritative and paternalistic traditions, it might be threatening to question the very traditions that, they might argue, are holding society together. And even when access is granted, it is possible that researchers would internalise those (authoritative) traditions. When discussing the political situation in Rwanda, Clark (2013:38), for example, warns that it is dangerous 'to internalise the logic of intimidation (inspired by a particular worldview), which means that many of us (meaning researchers) self-censor'. Those who do not internalise the environment of fear may instead swing to the other extreme of power imbalance behaviour, where the researcher is perceived

63

or considers himself or herself as of a superior civilisation than the researched. A balance must be struck between conducting studies that (may be seen to) internalise either the logic of colonialism of the Western world or that of intimidation in some parts of Africa. But as shall be shown in Chapter 7, researchers need to be clear about the methodology of structuration quadrant that defines their research.

Ontology-in-situ: There is also the inability for individuals leading institutions to separate themselves from the very institutions they lead and this is consistent with Thomson's (2004) assessment of most African leaders. This, to some extent, is a repercussion of Stones' (2005) strong structuration, which places an emphasis on *ontology-in-situ*. Such an emphasis is observable in some African leaders' inability to distinguish the concreteness of their persons with the impersonal institutions that they lead. Viewed in this way, not only are attempts to understand and scrutinise structures framed and aimed at people's personas, they are also viewed and perceived as attempts to expose the frailty of the individuals at the top of institutions. Without professional, political and emotional maturity/intelligence (Goleman et al. 2013), it is possible that decreasing fear pushing agents to scrutinise their institutions may resort to clashes between structure and agency, prompting a self-defence response from those representing structures instead of self-scrutiny. Self-scrutiny is not about personal attacks aimed at leaders but instead about institutions, in the same way that Giddens uses it when he talks about 'institutional reflectivity' (Beck et al. 1994).

Context: The issue of context is drawn from discussions and defence that certain African leaders and academics mount to justify what they claim to be context specific ideologies or philosophies and, therefore, rejecting Western-based concepts as 'out of context' by branding them as 'foreign' and 'colonial'. This ethical issue is highly crucial as it has the potential to unravel this entire publication, which essentially uses a 'foreign' concept (duality of structures) in a completely different context

(Africa). Given its seriousness, which warrants a discussion of equal measure, the next chapter is devoted to exploring this issue under the theme of 'cross-context studies'.

Analysis: Once ontological as well as epistemological issues have been articulated, we are faced not only with ethical issues that have been answered, in part, in this chapter and the next. One is also faced with the choice of a consistent data analysis strategy that reveals the extent to which a field (nations, schools, universities, hospitals, businesses, media, governmental and non-governmental organisations…) is on the path to duality of structures through increasing institutional self-scrutiny and decreasing fear on the part of the population or members of any field. It might be useful to start considering (critical) discourse analysis.

It is essential to re-familiarise with the discussion towards the end of Chapter 1, in order to fully grasp the coherence that discussion has with (critical) discourse analysis. In a nutshell, the argument that led to proposing *increasing self-scrutiny* and *decreasing fear* was based on the philosophical concept that privileged a shared implication between structure and agency in the shaping and reshaping of social reality. This was deemed to be a credible way forward, given a long history of broken trust that both structure and agency had shown over the years. Conceptual frameworks such as the *conditions, commitment, contributions and competence* of Mizrahi and Rosenthal (2001) and the *shared reality* of Echterhoff et al. (2009), were brought in to make the case for how duality of structures can be operationalised.

The right kind of communication in the formation of shared reality that is shaped as a result of duality of structures is essential. The duo *increasing self-scrutiny and decreasing fear,* therefore, serve as synchronised pedals that structure and agency use to cycle back and forth to allow shared social phenomenon to emerge. In this sense, we are not only concerned with the way communication unfolds for its own sake but importantly with how it works to construct genuine duality of structures inspired social realities. Foucault (1972) believed that language can help produce the objects it claims to describe. On that basis, critical discourse analysis is useful because

> critical discourse analysts go beyond the rhetorical and technical analysis of language to explore its social and political setting, uses and effects. They see language as crucial to ways that power is reproduced, legitimised and exercised within social relations and institutions (Tonkiss 2012:408).

Ultimately, data analysis will follow from how people come to know and how they communicate what they claim to know, given the *decreasing fear* and *self-scrutiny* modes that they are in. It is possible, though beyond the scope of this publication, to imagine a multiplicity of analysis strategies based on data from African art, stories, narratives, proverbs, etc.

Chapter 4

Double de-contextualisation:
a methodological myth or reality?

Abstract:

Journalistic reports during the November 2013 visit of the British Prime Minister David Cameron to China echoed one view of Chinese society (and perhaps of any other society) that Britain is a nice country to travel to and study in. Though this was meant to highlight Britain's 'diminishing' influence on the world stage, it can be argued that British universities are renowned worldwide and so are other universities in Europe, North America and why not Africa and Asia as shall be briefly alluded to in the next chapter. Yet there is a sense within communities whether in Asia, Africa or elsewhere, that one needs to go somewhere else to get quality education. In the same way, it can also seem as if one is at the centre of intellectual ideas to which the rest of the world gravitates. When intellectual concepts are said to be of a particular setting, they can be rejected by others under the same pretext and, hence, diminish their usefulness. We unquestionably either hand over or hold onto intellectual spaces. This chapter attempts to engage with underlying philosophical and methodological issues related to the complexity of cross-context studies, ownership as well as application of knowledge or theories that may seem close and yet removed from us, or vice versa.

Introduction

This chapter discusses and takes a position with regard to what is termed here as 'double de-contextualisation' (particularly when engaged in academic research with implications on cross-context studies). It begins with a brief definition of the central term(s) of reference. The following section provides a backdrop of instances when 'double de-contextualisation' may be prevalent and identifies some emergent issues, two of which are the stability and limitedness of knowledge. In the subsequent section, an analysis of possible types of knowledge or theories within social research when thinking about 'double de-contextualisation' in a complex world is given. It uses primary and secondary knowledge distinction to refer to various theoretical concepts in social research. This analysis leads to the identification of one academic, Pierre Bourdieu; and an attempt to locate his *secondary* theoretical concepts within complexity is made. What follows is an analysis, positioning and perhaps a didactically empowering presentation of arguments that can be used with regard to 'double de-contextualisation'.

Defining the term (s) of reference and rationale

This section explains what is meant by 'double de-contextualisation' here. According to the Oxford English Dictionary, 'to contextualise' means to place something into context. McCormarck et al (2002:96) define context as 'the physical environment in which practice takes place'. This definition is one-sided since it focuses only on *practice,* and as a result leaves out *theory* which also has its context. De-contextualisation is used then to mean when practice or practitioners are taken out of their contexts. There is also the reality of when a theory is taken out of its original context not simply by someone wanting to grasp it and in the process coming up with incorrect interpretations or distortions as is sometimes the case (Merizow 1997) but mainly by a researcher, who uses a given theory on a separate set of people or practitioners who do not constitute the original constituency from which the theory or intellectual idea was derived in the first place. In this instance, you end up with both theory and the new set of people (practitioners) the theory is being applied to taken out of their respective contexts, hence the phrase 'double de-contextualisation'. This entire publication is to some degree trapped in a 'double de-contextualisation' debate since it uses the concept of duality of structures by British sociologist Antony Giddens and applies it in an African context. It is hoped that the discussions in this chapter will give this work, and others facing the same issues, some ammunition to justify its legitimacy.

Concerns about theories of knowledge, what social reality is and how we come to know it, will continue to preoccupy those with an interest to understand their surroundings. Such interest could lead to research findings that are often discussed as part of researchers' (be it philosophers, sociologists etc.) theories some of which make it to conferences, symposia, publications and university lecture rooms. The view here is that those concerns, relating specifically to how and why we use what are provisionally termed *'context specific ideas'* to research our professional world, are not spelled out clearly in one piece. This is not to say that significant and perhaps ground-breaking attempts have not been made before. Reiterating an earlier argument by Smith (1999), as well as giving it a personal convincing account, Sikes (2006), for example, calls for a rethink of current methodologies that continue to hinder indigenous knowledge and methodologies from emerging. Owing to their pertinence, some of Sikes' recommendations will be rehearsed here.

Briefly though, Pat Sikes' paper is crucial in that it not only justifies the interest of a Westerner researching indigenous contexts but also makes one put into context an increased mobility in cross-context studies, as indicated in the abstract of this chapter. Drawing from her own higher education teaching experience, the paper is focused on what a university lecturer should do when teaching methodologies especially to those with 'otherness' status and, most importantly, questions the domineering nature of previous emancipatory methodologies that claim to give voice to the marginalised.

69

However, the paper seems one-sided in that the author's admission of the relevance of the decolonising methodologies movement is outweighed by an overemphasis on the need for 'othering' language of inclusion to promote marginalised voices in the world of research. The paper does not seem to articulate what positionality a student (indigenous or not) should take with regard to theories and contexts that may seem close and yet distant or vice versa. The concept of 'otherness' is also left unexamined, which only strengthens traditional assumptions about the sort of people who are being referred to. Without committing this chapter to queer theory traditions, which keep just about anything open to questioning (Creswell 2007), it is essential that the deconstruction process embedded in the narrative of 'decolonising methodologies' also provides a convincing deconstruction of concepts such as 'otherness'.

It is the view here that cross-context methodological issues need to be seen against a backdrop of (myth or reality?) of 'double de-contextualisation' and complexity, which affects *all* researchers. This chapter also aims to contribute to the need to rehearse ideas which can then be used to justify various (academic) writings of 'foreign' students, even 'home' students or those engaged in studying 'foreign' ideas in their 'home' universities.

When (double) de-contextualisation is most common

This section sets the scene for when 'double de-contextualisation' might be prevalent and discusses some initial issues that ensue. 'Double de-contextualisation' then might be described as a typical problem associated with novices in their early years' experience of researching their social and professional world. On a personal level, it will certainly take some years of research experiences before I am able to prove or disprove such a hypothesis. However, for colleagues in a similar position, and even for seasoned researchers humble enough to admit it, the questions of contextualisation and de-contextualisation of theories and research target populations are a real philosophical, as well as methodological, issue to grapple with. I will summarise a section of my previous publication to illustrate how complex 'contexts' are:

> I am from the Democratic Republic of the Congo (DRC), with a Christian background, French speaking, with two degrees in Philosophy and Theology obtained from Urbaniana University and Middlesex University. Both degrees were taught through the medium of English respectively in Uganda and London, UK. With a Masters degree in leadership and management in education, I am currently pursuing a doctoral degree in education with Sheffield Hallam University. I am using some of the theoretical frameworks that I have learnt, most of which are Western ideas, to research professional practice in the DRC (Elonga Mboyo 2015b).

A 'double de-contextualisation' critique would question the link that these frameworks have on the DRC context. There is nothing intentionally glaring here to be self-indulgent about but this biographical extract unmasks the multiplicity of contexts that we, as researchers, or any other person for that matter, are immersed in and perhaps the difficulty of exclusively predicating certain ideas we hold to one of the following: religion, traditional culture, modern culture, African concepts, European concepts, DRC, Uganda etc. To echo Abrahamsen (2003:206), the hybridity of (postcolonial) societies should not amount to disowning one's origins but accepting that 'local identities are not exhaustive and that appeals to fixed identities can contain their own dangers'.

Talk of (double) de-contextualisation is particularly common in parts of Africa or (political as well as intellectual) quarters that legitimately continue to assert their African/black identity as a way of subverting colonial and post-colonial forms of domination. Both demagogues and genuine patriotic

71

leaders/academics draw from an intellectual idea that defines black subjects as subjective entities who need:

> to remain true to ourselves as black learners who know ourselves more than the others who claim to know us better. It is to remain in touch with our holistic selves as African subjects of learning and creators of knowledge. It is to challenge Eurocentric mimicry and the seduction to become white (*or use Eurocentric concepts* – my Italics) in (*the African context* – my italics) the imperialist Western academy (Dei 2014:171).

The title *Linking Higher Education and Economic Development,* where Pillay (2010) analyses the implications of three successful systems (Finland, South Korea and the state of North Carolina in the United States of America) for Africa would struggle to pass the Eurocentric mimicry test. Modern Western democracy, for example, would be seen as a 'foreign' concept that cannot work in an African context, unless it is given its fitting African definition by none other than Africans themselves. Wiseman (2002:4), for example, notes that:

> In trying to assess the relative importance of internal and external pressures a large majority of academic observers, particularly those who are African, have concluded that it has been the internal pressures which have played a major role and that external developments have, at most, contributed relatively modestly.

A theory that is used to understand Africa needs to have been developed by an African in mind, as the Journal reviewer of the first chapter states: 'Why not use a theory produced by an Afrocentric theorist, like Molefi Asante, instead of one produced by Giddens, who certainly was not African in mind'. While the advice to 'preserve a creative tension' (Appaudurai 2009:50) between a European mimicry leading into appropriating imperialist practices and a domineering arrogance that sees no way other than that in 'which the coloniser is in the colonised' (Sykes 2013 citing Geertz 1973), should be followed, further clarity is needed to the debate.

The above observations and now the slogan 'African solutions to African problems' can be used opportunistically by both overstretched foreign governments, who cannot continuously provide resources that their own increasingly nationalistic electorates desperately need (Castle 2011), and the elites (representatives of structures) of African governments whose 'sovereign nation' mantra is often evoked to give them the space to define, perhaps singlehandedly and without the cooperation of the population, their African versions of democracies. In their 'sovereign nation' mantra, they disguise their desires to be national guardians, who 'get their position and power from the fact that only they are capable of interpreting tradition's ritual truth. Only they can decipher the real meanings of the sacred texts or the other symbols involved in the communal rituals' (Giddens 2002:41/42). Placing Africans at the heart of African problem-solving initiatives is also about recognising the fact that, in the modern age of increased technology and cross-boundary communication, our identities are a mix of different factors as illustrated in the above diary extract. Hence, an insular African context that needs to resist external theories and concepts needs to be reviewed.

Despite the complexity that we as subjects and the ideas that we produce are in, we still worry about pinning ideas down and getting things contextually right. Even if one disputed the notion of whether subjects produce ideas or ideas run through subjects, it would still seem legitimate to ask whether those ideas running through subjects are the product of specific contexts in their past or a product of a complex mix of variables. I am wary of the view that, despite acknowledging the problem with objective claims in social research, there is still a tendency that we, and ideas that any researcher uses, are or should be drawn from what can be termed as 'cleanly objective' sources, uncontaminated by

73

any other variables or 'contexts', to use a less positivistic term. It will come as no surprise by now that this chapter favours the idea of limited knowledge, but with the caveat that "one should realise that the claim that we cannot have complete knowledge does not imply that anything goes. 'Limited' knowledge is not equivalent to 'any' knowledge" (Cilliers, 2005:260). Echoing the view of complexity theorists, Cilliers goes on to demand that the inevitability of the tension and difficulty we are in when producing knowledge be recognised, demonstrated and talked about. The biggest challenge then is to do so without compromising the paramount requirement for 'our work to be taken seriously and perceived as convincing' (Mason, 1996:165).

Looking back at the above autobiographical extract, asking anyone in such a situation to recognise and respond to 'double de-contextualisation' can be interpreted at different levels. There is first the level of the heart/emotions. Such a level would ask rhetorical emancipatory questions, such as: 'why can't I use any idea I want to?' and 'am I being held back?' These questions are legitimate but they should only be a starting point, which leads to further questions. The second level then is the reflexivity level, which would not see oneself as being arbitrarily prevented from the use of certain concepts, which would run contrary to world class status and an outreach embrace of most 21st century higher education institutions, but recognise that we are all caught up in the world of complexity requiring reflexivity. From this perspective then, even the most obvious 'home-made' concepts, developed by your typical African, French, English and German philosopher or sociologist, are caught up in the complex world. The following section attempts to categorise knowledge or concepts, which should lead to the identification of a key anthropologist and sociologist (Pierre Bourdieu) whose, arguably complexity-bound, ideas have had a significant influence on other people's academic pursuits.

Knowledge and context: between durability and complexity/temporality

This section distinguishes between primary or conceptual knowledge, as opposed to secondary or empirical concepts within social science research, hence sidestepping the traditional positivist versus non-positivist knowledge discourse. The intention in coming up with some form of labelling is not to create another theoretical framework or set any order of importance in knowledge but to provide a terminology or a glossary that can be used when thinking about the justification of the use of certain theoretical concepts in the methodological (myth or reality?) 'double de-contextualisation' debate. Needless to say that the labelling could only be achieved by way of analysis of what currently exists as bodies of knowledge available to be 'contextualised or de-contextualised' as the title of the chapter suggests, and not based on any first-hand fieldwork.

Primary or conceptual concept

In organisational literature, Ribbins and Gunter (2002) have identified a form of knowledge, among others, called 'conceptual', which I referred to here as 'primary' knowledge that is arguably not based on specific contexts.

The conceptual knowledge domain, according to the above authors is concerned with the clarification of (leadership) terms or concepts without recourse to empirical data from specific settings. Philosophy, in general, and some of its branches such as metaphysics, in particular, can be said to produce knowledge that can be categorised as 'purely' conceptual. Sociological concepts such as *structuration theory* of Antony Giddens, that Stones (2005) calls *ontology-in-general,* also form part of conceptual knowledge given its trans-situational character. Computer generated artificial intelligence can be included for its claimed independence from specific contexts (Nishida 2008) although saying that is problematic in itself. Making it to this list, you could argue, are concepts emerging from reviews of other people's works. The reviews add conceptual categories onto other works without recourse to direct empirical research, even though they too (might) depend on earlier empirical research by other authors. It is within reason to imagine that most organised educational subjects with a formal body of knowledge (Freidson 2001) would have literature reviews of some sort and some familiar examples when thinking about educational leadership research and organisational analysis: Ribbins and Gunter (2002) as already mentioned, and Burrell and Morgan (1979).

Empirical or secondary knowledge

In contrast then, much of the work of empirical researchers, such as anthropologists or ethnographers, for example, is based on carrying out fieldwork, which involves going out, whether this is done virtually or by use of any media from the comfort of one's office or physically uprooting oneself from a familiar setting to another setting. It is inextricably linked to context and subjectivity. Secondary knowledge is used here to refer to theories emerging from empirical studies.

The next section will develop the argument on when to use either primary or secondary concepts. The focus for now is on how the French anthropologist and sociologist Pierre Bourdieu can serve as an example to demonstrate/illustrate the complexity of empirical or secondary knowledge. Anyone familiar with Bourdieu's works will be amazed at the creativity of concepts such as habitus, capital, field, doxa, structure, agency, and others, to describe the materiality and symbolic representation of the social world (better to say French society if we are to stick with the theme of contextualisation), as a result of his empirical or secondary knowledge based studies in France. Let us briefly focus on the theme of 'symbolic capital' as a result of his analysis of the French state (1994). The discussion below moves from an analysis of Bourdieu's studies based in one state (France) to another (Algeria) and back to argue for a link between ideas emerging from multiple settings.

Bourdieu and the state of France

From observations of the way the French state and people related to some of its conventions, especially the field of orthography of words, Bourdieu concluded that such laws became the norm (for identity and prestige) for subjects, who would display an agentic force in the form of protests if an attempt to change those laws that have come to define 'the categories of perception' (Bourdieu 1994:8) were made. The categories of perception are what he would call symbolic capital, which relates to other forms of capital, such as economic capital as physical force and field of power in relation to the formation of a state. Though Bourdieu uses these concepts only in his later works, we need to remind ourselves that his earlier work emerging from field studies in Algeria provides a pivotal backdrop.

Bourdieu and the state of Algeria

Much earlier, Pierre Bourdieu had asserted his credentials as an anthropologist after his successful first publication entitled *La Sociologie de l'Algerie* in 1958. Ethnographic data from his fieldwork offered an insight into the lives of Kabyle peoples, power relations and, most importantly, the interactions between the state (French colonisers) and their subjects. Driven by an economic desire in the interest of their country, the French resorted to forced (or voluntary) displacement of Algerians, in huge numbers, to ensure that the colonisers gained access to the land was. Given the intensity and harshness of the colonial and Algerian war of independence, Bourdieu (1958) captures the mood of resignation among Algerians saying that Algerians inevitably became reconciled and accustomed to a state of existence that was rather vegetative, a sort 'symbolic void' resulting from losing the resources that signified their cultural identity and pride. Despite his failure to use the words habitus, fields and especially 'symbolic capital', there is a strong argument to suggest that Bourdieu's intellectual work in Algeria influenced our conception of practice being the result of various habitual schemas and dispositions (habitus), combined with resources (capital), being activated by certain structured social conditions (field) which they, in turn, belong to and variously reproduce and modify (Bourdieu 1984).

The point here is far from questioning Bourdieu's subjectivity and authorship, but rather to highlight that his original sociological thinking is entangled in the multiplicity of contexts. It is possible that a present-day French researcher would feel free to use Bourdieu's concepts, assuming closeness with them based on a predicate that Bourdieu is naturally French. Similarly, the use of Bourdieu's concepts, such as habitus, capital and others, may be challenged when used in an African context, for example, on the grounds that he is French and that most of his concepts were fully developed after research conducted on France. However, as presented above, what is close may seem far removed from today's French researcher and what seems removed from an African context may indeed be close to it if one considers that Bourdieu's theories could have originated from a context other than France. It could be concluded that the idea of 'otherness' has to do with people '*out-there*' as much as it is to do with '*us-here*'. The main implication of this observation is that it would be academically, politically and culturally naïve to dismiss other approaches to life, based on the assumption that nation state contexts are impervious and bounded. The pertinent question is then, what do we do with secondary or empirical knowledge that is rooted in the complexity of contexts? The following section attempts to offer some justified recommendations.

'Double de-contextualisation': a positioning

This section moves to analyse and suggest the approach to take with regard to the types of concepts or knowledge identified here when thinking or worrying about 'double de-contextualisation'.

a. How can we use primary concepts?

Echoing concerns by Schegloff (1997) when talking about the tendency for relativisation and perspectivalisation in cultural analysis, it could be argued that it is a misplacement to import indeterminacy into stable meanings that primary or conceptual knowledge carry. There are trans-situational ontological concepts and categorised knowledge domains through literature reviews that empower us to analyse and develop our understanding of social reality. It is not a distortion, therefore, to argue for stability of meaning when it might be claimed that 'all' knowledge is limited, tacitly configured (Polianyi 1966) and even most literature reviewers would always be clear about the provisionality of their conceptual frameworks. What is being argued here is that knowledge may be provisional, as new conceptual frameworks could render old ones redundant but they still remain stable, in so far as they do not depend on the relationship between the reviewer's framing and specific contexts, hence giving leverage for their use to anyone in any context as long as the concepts and aims of the study are clearly defined. To partly answer the question embedded in this chapter's title then, it would seem that 'double de-contextualisation' is a myth, particularly in relation to primary or conceptual knowledge that seems to have a cross-context durability, not to use stronger language of having an 'intrinsic' cross-context nature.

b. *How can we use secondary concepts?*

In the light of previous discussions, this section will suggest the different approaches that can be taken with regard to the use of secondary concepts. Those approaches will centre around four key ideas: subjectivity, innovation, developmental learning and emergence of local theories.

1. *Subjectivity*: as already mentioned in the structure/agency debate, subjectivity is a fact of life. An essential part of that subjectivity is about not dogmatically rooting oneself in a situation but also about examining and questioning (some might

say 'thinking outside the box') one's surroundings. This is the power of reflexivity where humans recognise the world they live in and acknowledge that their perceptions are subject to that world. Personal trajectories are the familiar/subjective lenses through which we see the world. An African as a subject can consider himself or herself as closed off in his or her own world but the reality of modernisation and technological advancement is that we are increasingly becoming citizens of the world. In phenomenological research, Levering (2007:215) argues that the "'I' and the 'world' are inextricably intertwined" and drawing from Heidegger's (1954) concept of *Dassein* (man in-the-world), he goes on to say that "human existence implies that man is not only bodily in-the-world, but is also projected in time. Man is not only 'now', but he is a unity of past, present *and future*" (217). Hence, even if some might think that their past and present have been sealed off from the rest of the world, there is no guarantee that the future will be.

There are several ways of looking at Levering's observations, which could justify the use of 'foreign' concepts when analysing and wanting to engage with social phenomena in an African context. The autobiographical diary extract shows the multiplicity of contexts that we inhabit and that it is only through such previously acquired experiences, language and theories that we can seek to understand the world. Another way of illustrating how reflexivity reflects through subjectivity is to say that the same failed past leadership practices on the African continent are having a negative effect on the present and the people who embody that negative feeling want (or seek out) alternatives (theory and practice) to have a different experience in-their-future-world .

2. *Innovation*: Lash (1994) uses the impact specialised consumption has had on the way products reach customers. Firms are now producing smaller batches and at the same time having to widen the array of products. In the same line of thinking, it can be argued that, due to globalisation, Africans are interconnected subjects. Despite the fact that the right for

information is still being curtailed in some places, technological advancement through the internet means that people are not going to be satisfied with one (failed) way of doing things. Innovation through reflexivity is what is needed here. From the mind-set of innovation, concepts do not rule themselves out because they are 'foreign'. Rather they belong to an array of resources that can be used to diversify services and be more effective in solving problems ethically and sustainably. Concepts rule themselves out only if they are not yielding any results on the ground after a genuine effort to get them working as 'agents reformulate and use rules and resources in a variety of combinations in order to innovate' (Lash 1994:119).

3. *Developmental learning.* Unlike primary concepts, secondary concepts have so far been presented as not having 'epistemic independence'. 'Epistemic independence' here is the characteristic of some concepts to be transhistorical but not 'ahistorical and independent from the field of concrete human experience socio-political concern and action' (Papastephenou 2001:300). However, if there was no such awareness already, the writing of Freire (1970) is a reminder that human action, including research, should be guided towards empowerment and changing practices. This consequentialist approach embraces theory, more specifically secondary concepts, with a presumption that they have not only some form of 'structure' beyond the local contexts but also for the potential they have to provide learning opportunities for those interacting with them in other settings. Instead of placing emphasis on what sometimes seems to be a purely theoretical distinction between primary and secondary concepts, rather the focus would rather be on the single, double and triple loop practical learning (Tobert 1999) that individuals, as well as organisations, gain as they engage with secondary concepts.

People have visions and strategies, which could include dreams about creating something new or experimenting with alternative strategies. These strategies could be of a different context but would provide several single, double and triple loop learning for me, you and others involved in the learning. The use of the concept of duality of structures, as is the case in this publication and other attempts to use secondary concepts/knowledge in various contexts, can legitimately be carried forward with the intention of adding to a researcher's personal learning as he or she engages in the research, the learning as a team process of conducting an enquiry and how the enquiry contributes to knowledge.

4. *Emergence of local theories*: In a positivist one cap fits all approach, data collected from various contexts would often be used to test some generalisable theories. Glaser and Strauss (1999) reversed this overshadowing dominance of quantitative over qualitative research by showing that data can be used to construct rather than to test a theory. This grounded theory approach to research is not only decolonising in relation to qualitative versus quantitative, but also a blatant admission of the importance that local contexts and their data play in the emergence of theories.

Sikes (2006:350) has attributed this decolonising egalitarian approach to:

• The impact of postmodernism and post-structuralism and the increasing acceptance of multiple realities and alternative world views, incorporating an awareness of how, as individuals, we each can and do occupy a multiplicity of subject positions;

• Ever-increasing commitment to the recognition and realization of social justice, equity and equality for all peoples, underpinned by social models of differences, society and the world;

• Enhanced sensitivity to the role of discourse in constructing and framing identities and relationships;

•Various consequences of globalisation and of improved communications and technologies, which have had the effect of shrinking the world and bringing people from far-flung places into closer contact with each other;

• The money-making activities and expansionist, philanthropic, equalitarian and democratizing ambitions of western universities as manifested in terms of increasing overseas student numbers both at home and via various outreach and distance learning programmes;

• The research-related and educative work of non-governmental organisations and development agencies;

• Growing numbers of 'new' scholars and researchers who themselves come from 'other' cultures, communities and backgrounds or who are differently abled; and of course,

• Guilt.

Conclusion:

It is legitimate to recognise the power imbalance that historical events, such as colonisation, have had on the way that we perceive knowledge and research. This chapter does not deny such imbalance but recognises the complexities of knowledge generation in an increasingly globalised world. The analysis has led to the identification of what could be termed as 'an epistemological circus' (see figure below) that both the traditional 'others' and 'non-others' can use to locate and justify various writings, commentaries and research projects.

The figure attempts to summarise the discussion in this chapter. It shows the cross context student, researcher or anyone who still has what could be called personal or cultural values, knowledge, and methodologies plunged into a globalised knowledge circus. In that knowledge circus, there are concepts that are primary and others that are secondary. Primary concepts, as discussed earlier, are trans-situational and have an epistemic independence and they can be used or be applied to study and understand various situations. The secondary concepts are where theories are used for various reasons and purposes, such as: subjectivity, innovation, developmental learning and emerging local theories. This framework is certainly not final but it has ideas that can be used to justify various cross context studies.

With regard to the use of structuration theory in this publication, I use it here first as a *primary* concept. When framed as a *secondary* concept, I use it as part of my subjectivity and as an attempt for innovation to solve an enduring problem as indicated by reviewer 1 in the first chapter. Structuration theory is, as I argue in Chapter 3, a very African concept otherwise known as Ubuntu.

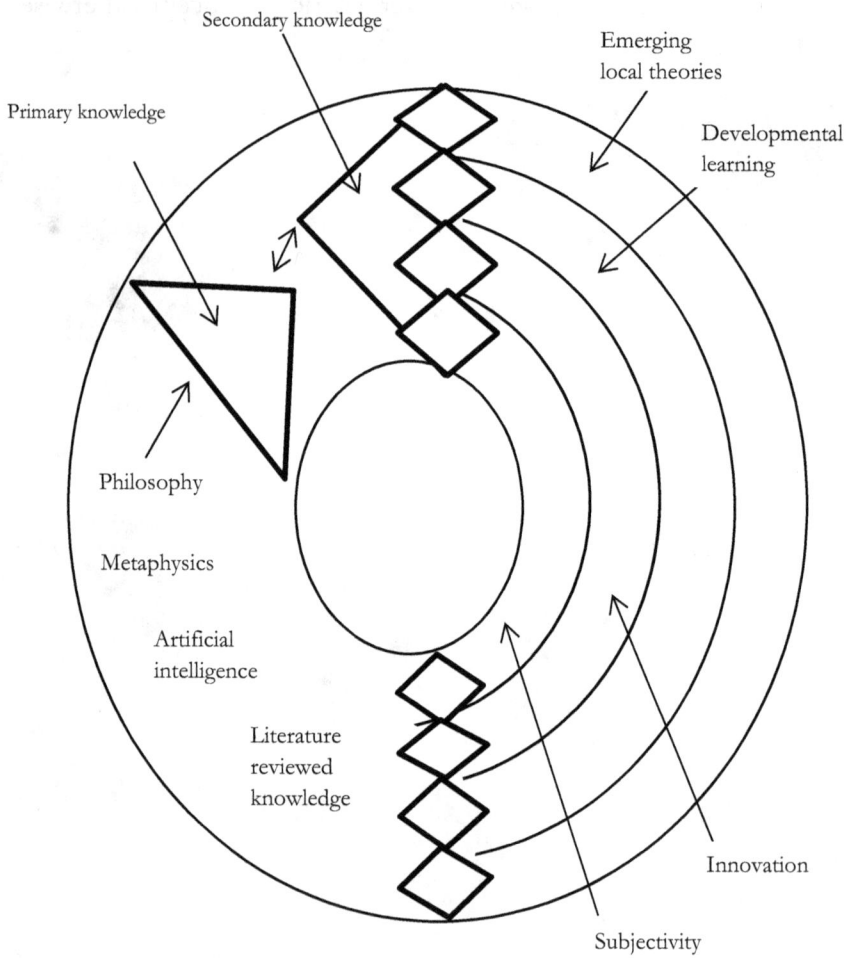

Secondary knowledge

Emerging
local theories

Primary knowledge

Developmental
learning

Philosophy

Metaphysics

Artificial
intelligence

Literature
reviewed
knowledge

Innovation

Subjectivity

Chapter 5

Higher education in the DRC and Sub-Saharan Africa: duality of structures in action

Abstract

A country's higher education can be seen as pivotal for human resource capacity building and stimulation of ideas for economic prosperity. Having been asked to help to formulate a programme of study for a potential upcoming university/higher education institute in the Democratic of Republic of Congo (DRC), a lot of questions, not least the relevance of a programme of the kind that was beginning to emerge for a post-conflict state, came to mind. This triggered a stepping back and considering of certain important issues beforehand. This chapter, therefore, reviews challenges that universities in the DRC and Sub-Saharan Africa face, analyses the current thinking about "prestigious/world-class" universities and proposes local interactions, professionalism, lifelong education and quality assurance as the building blocks of curriculum development that sets the direction for universities/higher education institutes in the DRC and perhaps elsewhere in Africa. In retrospect, the new direction being proposed here can be framed as a practical example for putting the duality of structures into action.

Introduction

This chapter begins with a brief overview of the state of higher education in the Democratic Republic of the Congo (DRC). This is followed by an outline of various non-exhaustive challenges that universities in the DRC and perhaps Sub-Saharan Africa face. In the search for excellence, a critical analysis of some internationally 'agreed' standards is undertaken, in order to highlight what could be the strengths and limitations of such social constructs. This is followed by a presentation of the 2008-2009 objectives of differentiated higher education in the DRC that I was able to gather. These objectives are then analysed in terms of their strengths and limitations in the overall need for a DRC or African-based construction of excellence.

Extracts from my reflective diary, which took shape alongside the process of drafting a higher education programme of study in response to a colleague's request, will be used. The extracts will include the use of subjective/objective pronouns and possessive adjective such as "I", "my" and "me" to retain their originality and personalised nature. Taking all into consideration, the paper leads to proposing a framework that a university/higher education institution, in an environment such as the DRC (or others with similar realities), could draw from when thinking about curriculum/programme of study design and the direction of higher education institutes without jeopardising quality. The key aspects of the proposed framework, that shall be elaborated on later, are: local interactions, professionalism, lifelong education and quality assurance. The diversity of situations and the justification we all have for varying degrees of discernment mean that any given framework will not touch on absolute minutiae and it is possible that the reader may come away with more questions than answers. The view here is that such questions are quintessential, since they encourage further reflections on the adequacy and suitability of envisaged solutions in different contexts.

DRC universities and their problems

Higher education is being perceived as an essential component for nations to be competitive in the knowledge society (Albatch 2007) and meet environmental challenges (Brock 2012). Hence, questions surrounding curriculum and overall leadership of higher education institutions become necessary (Bolden et al. 2009).

The DRC's higher education is divided into three parts: universities, higher technical institutes and higher pedagogical institutes. The total number of higher education institutes came to 776 by the end of 2009, of which 384 were public against 392 that were being privately owned/run (Unesco 2010). Unesco also notes that there were/are more higher technical institutes than universities and higher pedagogical institutes nationally, whether public or private. Between them, they shared a student population of 379,867. The country is enormous in terms of size and the total population is estimated to be over 60 million people, which may be similar to some European states with less higher education institutions. One could conclude, therefore, that the university and higher education sector in the DRC, like anywhere else (Jonasson 2008), is growing/expanding/evolving but not without its problems, which are discussed below.

Jeongwoo (2013) argues that most universities in Africa, with the exception of some in Egypt, Kenya and South Africa, cannot compete and their chances of becoming world-class universities are slim unless dramatic action is taken. It is understandable that universities in the DRC were not included on that list. While others might see this non-inclusion as consistent with successive governments' shunning of their responsibilities (Titeca and De Herdt 2011), a long past history of conflict may be used to excuse current difficulties as the following comment by Teferra and Albatch (2004:22) might be (perhaps mistakenly) interpreted "… Somalia, Angola, and the Democratic Republic of Congo (DRC), have lost university-level institutions as the result of political turmoil and are trying to rebuild a postsecondary sector". Regardless of the causes, there remain difficulties that need to be faced. The DRC state's absence in the primary and secondary education sectors (De Hert et al. 2012) which has seen a huge decline in state funding is a trend that did not spare higher education and/or universities. The longstanding underinvestment in this sector has led to what

Mokonzi (2010:8) calls "a recruitment freeze on teaching staff". According to Mokonzi, 61% of all higher education staff do administrative jobs rather than teaching.

Many unqualified teachers are also responsible for the erosion of the quality of education, according to the Organisation for Economic Cooperation and Development (2008). Quality, however, is only an implied concern in the list of challenges that the then minister for higher education and universities identified, prefacing a 2008-2009 Unesco annual report on the state of higher education in the DRC (Unesco 2010). Those concerns are: state absence, proliferation of higher education institutes, ageing academic staff, poor infrastructure, lack of scientific equipment/laboratories/libraries, inadequate funding and poor governance. If we compare these with the challenges universities in Africa face, then one begins to see that most problems are not limited to the DRC (Amonoo-Neizer 1998; Teferra and Albatch 2004).

Amonoo-Neizer (1998), for example, identifies the problems African universities face as ranging from reduced funding, increased university student populations affecting quality, staffing and poor or inexistent research innovations, to the overall relevance of the university as an institution given growing unemployment rates, which requires "continuing curriculum review and modification" (306). There may have been some improvement since Amonoo-Neizer made the foregoing observations. However, the most recent one by Brock and Alexiadou (2013) is that Sub-Saharan Africa is the least developed region (in terms of education) in the world, which means that universities still need to do more to play an effective role in the knowledge society (Albatch 2007).

Responding adequately to the above challenges or, in other words, ensuring that quality is matched by the quantitative expansion of higher education institutions, especially in the DRC, is essential. Amonoo-Neizer (1998) suggests adaptation, transformation, reformation and revitalisation. What these concepts mean in terms of curriculum design is not clearly

89

articulated. Besides, the concepts tell us not only about the need for quality but they can also reveal different aspirations that universities have, including established ones in other parts of the world.

In terms of aspirations, they may be best represented in two poles. On the one hand, there are the "less credible" universities, which do not want to be or would argue that they are not failing. On the other end of the spectrum is the "world-class" university status (Jeongwoo 2013) that does not come without personal, collective sacrifices and hard decisions to make. Mukonyora (2007:222) uses the term "successful universities", suggesting there is a staged trajectory in the overall drive to achieve elite "world-class" status. It is also possible that Isabel Mukonyora uses the phrase "successful universities" to mean "world-class" universities. Whatever the stages, or rather the diversified and differentiated state of the higher education sector, the criteria for a university to be classed as "world-class" (Jeongwoo 2013), which are discussed shortly, seem desirable at face value. However, a critique of those standards is vital in establishing the relevance of a university programme of study, and the direction of higher education institutes in the DRC and Sub Saharan Africa, that do not or may never make it to the top, or thereabouts, of 'world-class' ranking but are still regarded as successful universities. The main question, therefore, that this chapter attempts to answer is: how do the DRC's and Sub-Saharan Africa's universities define their programmes of study to secure the success that would justify their future existence?

Rethinking current understanding of "Successful" or "world-class" universities

World-class universities
There is no unanimity as to what constitutes a "successful" or "world-class" university. However, based on global higher education rankings, Jeongwoo (2013) proposes four common features of those universities that seem to have propelled them

to the top. The first is the *international dimension,* which is often identifiable by the worldwide student population and outreach of the university. The second is the *intensity of research* that seems to co-exist with the activities of an increased number of top academics in any one "world-class" university. The third relates to the *technology and resources* that are not only made available prior to research activities but are also a by-product of their cutting edge research. The final characteristic is *genuine autonomy,* that is, free from outside control and interference in order for universities to engage in knowledge inquiries that seek the emancipation of mankind. With the exception of the last characteristic, which is necessary so that decision makers can act on the basis of an unbiased knowledge base, the discussion in the next section will focus on the other features in the context of universities in the DRC and the rest of Sub-Saharan Africa.

Rethinking the features/standards

The scale of "huge investment which presumably might mean taking assets from other segments of the national education system" (Jeongwoo 2013:243) needs sustained financial and political will. The view here is that, with or without those huge investments, it is possible to imagine that some universities in the world may have reached "world-class" status by their own measure. However, the fact that such institutions are not yet recognised as such may not only be down to a public relations matter, which would justify millions of dollars from those huge investments being rechannelled into website redesign, television and radio adverts by universities to raise their profiles (Brewer et al. 2002; Kittle 2000). It could be argued that the problem lies in the flawed ranking system and conceptualisation of prestigious universities.

Brock and Alexiadou (2013:154) state, perhaps without elaborating on their position, that "universities in this region (meaning Sub-Saharan Africa) and other poor developing countries are poorly served by the international obsession with university rankings". An anecdotal way of interpreting the above pertinent comment is to note the increasing number of African politicians who do little to improve their own universities but instead spend considerable sums of money supporting their children and relatives through those "first-class universities" out of Africa. This has pushed some to take a radical stance calling for a ban on African politicians schooling abroad (allafrica.com 2012). It may be financially unpopular and unpalatable for those "world-class" universities but a liberating policy nonetheless for millions of Africans. An alternative approach would be to put in place a reviewable moratorium on the children of parliamentarians, senators and African government officials seeking admission into Western primary, secondary schools and undergraduate courses, and only admit them at doctoral level after a test and if they can prove that they have done an undergraduate degree in their home countries.

Let us return to the problem that university ranking poses. While acknowledging the need for African universities to engage with the reality of globalisation in its technological, economic and cultural dimensions (Amonoo-Neizer 1998; Mukonyora 2007), it has to be said that the categorisation "world-class" is a social construct. The intention here is not to water down any agreed standards for defining what does or does not make a world-class university but instead to question the tendency to objectify not only the "world-class" university standards we set but also the ways of achieving those standards. In so doing, we forget that not only can success be defined differently but also that it can be arrived at through other ethically moral means. The editorial by Acedo (2012) in the *Prospects'* special issue alludes to this question when presenting the ideas of one of the contributors to the appealing nature of "world-class" education around the world. Acedo (2012:335) asks: "whose voice is being heard? Whose are not? Whose discourse is it that results in particular standards, benchmarks, and indicators?". These questions do not only highlight the fact that "world-class" university standards are socially constructed concepts, but that they also strengthen the case for universities in the DRC, and

92

Africa in general, to consider their positions and advance a coherent and credible discourse right from the conception of their programmes of study. The latter part of this chapter proposes one such discourse. However, for the sake of the argument, the immediate focus is on contextualising "world-class" university standards.

On the international nature of "world-class" universities, for example, Mukonyora (2007:222) advances a subtly nuanced view, arguing that "successful universities are those that take seriously the needs of the wider society they serve as part of building bridges between the local and the global". Seen in this way, a local university with local students can still have an international outlook and openness to it. The challenge for those defining the mission, purpose and setting up of programmes of study for universities/higher education, therefore, is to project an outward approach rather than be inward-looking. While this can lead to increased national, regional and international partnerships between universities, private sectors and foreign governments and organisations that are vital (Jeongwoo 2013), it opens up important horizons in terms of importing and exporting knowledge systems (Mukonyora 2007).

While "successful" or "world-class" universities need to be research intensive (Jeongwoo 2013), this factor is somehow linked to universities hiring "top academics". The necessity of having top academics whose knowledge and skills in advancing the cause of science in whatever field cannot be stressed enough here. However, global technological advancement, in the form of knowledge sharing through books and online internet-based publications, means that knowledge is no longer limited to the physical person inhabiting a specific institution. The challenge for universities in the DRC, therefore, is to improve the availability and accessibility of global as well as local knowledge through various media, in order perhaps to offset the brain-drain (Taferra and Albatch 2004) but, more importantly, to advance the vocation that Mukonyora (2007:223), citing Thomas

93

Aquinas (d.1274), sees in universities as "a place to learn about everything to enhance life in the created world".

Looking beyond the religious nature (created world) of Aquinas' world view, there is an issue with the idea of universities being a place where you learn about *anything* or *everything*. This is worrying and perhaps a utopia for those universities, especially in the DRC, that are faced with certain challenges, some of which have already been identified here. The lack of clarity around the above italicised word/concept can result in universities, in the DRC and elsewhere, setting themselves unrealistic expectations. While the idea of learning about *anything* is appealing, in terms of enquiry pushing the boundaries of previously acquired knowledge further and deeper, the need for formalised and specialist knowledge (Freidson 2001; Larson 1977) implies that universities need to have a clear and well-defined focus. Jeongwoo (2013:244) is therefore right in using the examples of Caltech and London School of Economics to point out that "universities need not be comprehensive in their academic missions or be outstanding in all fields". But even then, I would argue that such universities do not learn *just about anything* in their chosen fields. Learning about *anything* has to be seen in the context of learning being a lifelong enterprise (Coombs and Ahmed 1974; Van de Veen and Preece 2005). In this sense, life, as long as it lasts, is where we learn about *anything*. Universities/higher education institutes, then, become places that equip students with the necessary (analytical) skills to understand, improve and perhaps predict the social and natural world beyond the confines of university establishments.

To revisit an earlier concern, world-class university status seems to put universities in a *ranking* order rather than in a *pool*. Ranking orders seem to work in such a way that even universities that are performing well are not given their due consideration, as they may have been dislodged by others jostling for higher positions. Jeongwoo's (2013:239) example seems appropriate here to illustrate this problem:

Malaya University in Malaysia was ranked second highest, after China, among developing countries in 2004, but dropped from 121st to 201st (QS 2004, 2012). Therefore, while it appears that some developing countries desire to create one or more world-class universities, developed countries and a few developing countries are moving at a faster pace and taking actions to win the global competition.

It is outside the scope of this chapter to engage in a discussion about the Kantian transcendental argument or the Weberian concept of ideal-types. However, on the basis of the above citation, it is fair to argue that human experience is constituted in categories such as here and there, highest and lowest (Bristow 2002). Despite the fact that the ranking culture cannot be ignored, since it has generated rich discussions about excellence, comparisons and economic development, it is questionable on the grounds that it seems to have become a profit generating enterprise for both the rankers and their regulators (Robertson 2012).

The *pooling* approach seems more credible in that it recognises both the diversity in our approaches to creating knowledge and efforts made by numerous universities without making them feel second-class. To what extent universities integrate the above contextualised aspects of "world-class" university features will be the next focus, using the official objectives for higher education institutes in the DRC.

Official expectations of universities/higher education in the DRC

In parts of Africa, especially in the DRC, state absence in the education sector, in general, seems to have led to the proliferation of private higher education institutions (Unesco 2010) and such institutions may have their own regimes. In principle, however, the DRC's state and private higher education institutions have to adhere to certain mandatory objectives, which presumably impact on curriculum design and the direction they take. Those objectives are outlined and critiqued here, in order to take a position with regard to the direction universities in the DRC, and perhaps in Sub-Saharan Africa, should take.

Like most countries with a differentiated higher education system, this sector in the DRC is made up of universities, higher technical institutes and higher pedagogical institutes (Unesco 2010). Whatever the conceptualisations in terms of quality, the view here is that excellence does not pertain exclusively to universities and not to higher technical and pedagogical institutes. However, for anyone wanting to set up a higher education institute, or university, or convert from any one form to another, a coherent guide addressing the concerns raised here and enabling silent voices to be heard in the overall discourse about "world-class" education is necessary.

Based on Unesco's (2010:18-19) publication sanctioned by the DRC government, which I translate (from French to English) below, higher education institutes have specific objectives:

1. Universities: Their primary responsibility is for the training of *cadres de conception* in *all* aspects of national life and with immediate relevance to the social and economic development of the country and secondly for the organisation of scientific research that aims to solve the country's specific problems and align with the evolution of science and technology.

2. Higher technical institutes: These are responsible for the training of *cadres spécialisés* and *intermédiaires* [senior executives and middle managers] both in applied sciences and arts, as well as encouraging artistic talents in line with the country's adaptation of modern information technologies, and

3. Higher pedagogical institutes: They aim to train teachers who, in a general and specialised way, will work to improve the

96

quality of education by integrating a rethink of people's roles in society and through the carrying out and publication of research.

Analysis

There are certainly various positive aspects from the above objectives that can be used to strengthen the case for excellence. The concern for national interests is high on the agenda here and so is a long-term approach that intends to cover *all* aspects of national life. The differentiated institutions also suggest that there is the awareness that *one size does not fit all* and that research is the engine for further innovation and economic development. It is, however, fair to say that these are not only aspirational goals but also partial, in that they highlight a three-way gap between these aspirational goals, current challenges and contextualised "world-class" standards.

Without repeating the problems that DRC's (Sub-Saharan) universities face, that are not redressed in the above objectives, it is necessary to consider how some of the aspirational goals for the DRC's higher education institutes may be counterproductive to the overall drive for excellence of the stated differentiated higher education system. For those grappling with essential questions about the relevance of any higher education programme in the DRC, they are bound to be even more confused about the definition of *all aspects* of national life. Here again, we are back to an earlier discussion about whether excellence can be defined only in terms of either *everything* or some specifically defined body of knowledge. Linked to this is the balancing act that might need to be negotiated between the highly prioritised national and international interests, in order to impress its own kind of national and international narrative of excellence. Until tangibly concerted efforts are made, in terms of investments in higher education, public or private universities in the DRC and Sub-Saharan Africa will have to rely on a workable approach/philosophy that enables them to do more with less, as it were. Taking the foregoing discussions into

97

account, below is an outline of an arguably manageable approach to achieving excellence, and perhaps writing a different African-based "world-class" university story. Given the limitations of current frameworks regarding "world-class" universities highlighted above, I posit this framework as a viable alternative. The tenets of the framework are local interactions, professionalism, lifelong education and quality assurance.

Proposed framework

Research elsewhere recognises the need for *planned for* and *emergent* approaches to universities/higher education institutes', curriculum design and management of universities that are arguably complex organisations. At the heart of such complexity, that must be anticipated even in the case of universities in the DRC, is the idea that agents (staff, administrators, etc.) "behave according to (their) own principles of local interactions" (Stacey 2000:42). While the local interactions may be very hard to penetrate, influence and regulate for existing universities that have had various individuals in and out of their institutions, that difficulty may be less so for smaller institutions in their early days. However, a more durable approach is necessary to turn the difficulty of complexity into an opportunity. This is why curriculum planning, and perhaps the overall conduct of business at higher education level, should be subjected to local interactions.

1. **Local interactions**: The internet and education mobility are empowering tools. One can just walk up to a renowned university or turn to google or any other search engine to get some tips on university curriculum and/or organisation that can be used in the DRC. While that is not necessarily a bad thing in itself, it only makes university organisation in the DRC and Africa as a whole more complex than such institutions already are (McRoy and Gibbs 2009; Stacey 2000). However, since one has to start somewhere in designing a higher education programme of study (see extract below), there has to be a

98

philosophical recognition and practical strategy that does not force ideas on people but subjects them to local scrutiny and interactions. Rather than it being a one-off act, the process of local interactions needs to be a continuous exercise of assimilation, enrichment, adaptation and innovation, as planned objectives come face to face with contextually emergent needs, realities and interpretations. Below is a diary extract to illustrate the importance of this point:

As part of my research in putting together a programme of study, I visited the webpage of the department of education of the University of Laval (2014). I realised the university ran a programme leading to an award of a certificate in professional and technical teaching which counts towards a baccalaureate qualification. The main objectives of this programme seemed appealing and perhaps relevant to the DRC. However, the importance of local subjects' interactions was felt when my discussions with those I considered local people began to question the implications of calling the award a "certificate" which for most people in the DRC refers to a primary school qualification. State Diploma is what you get after completing secondary education. A useful conversation followed on whether to adapt it to the context of the DRC and perhaps call it "Diplôme avancé" (higher diploma) or a "certificat d'études avancées" (certificate of higher studies).

Another way of underscoring the importance of local interactions (based on local needs) is in the area of research, which is the driving force for (world-class) universities. Let us take the example of research around 'water' in response to the needs of a particular African community. A research driven centre or university in an African community that does not have clean running water would prioritise research on drinking water treatment over waste water treatment. This is not a licence for flouting standards for sustainable development but an attempt to highlight the importance of research based on local interactions/needs.

Whilst one might encounter rigidity and opposition to innovations, local subjects embody historical and ontological conventions, which represent their interdependent identity with nature and the rest of the world. The emphasis here is more on the local subjects involved in the dialogue rather than the content of the discussions, even though the two overlap. In the knowledge society, Hargreaves (2003) has noted that, while good educational institutions may enjoy some autonomy, those deemed as failing were subjected to intense performance training. The danger, therefore, is to waive internal dialogue and local interactions to rebuild confidence in favour of intense performance training of staff (Ball 2008) in universities (in the DRC), in order to transform a region that is deemed the least poorly developed in terms of education (Bock and Alexiadou 2013). This must be carried out cautiously and avoid destroying archaeological heritage (Arazi 2009), resulting in a "tenser relationship between humans and nature" (Fu et al. 2007:7594) and significantly (or irreparably) disrupting people's ways of life, as well as damaging their health (Wang et al. 2013). In this new light, one only waives local interactions at the cost of a dialogue that is needed to build bridges with other knowledge systems and on many other levels. Therefore, setting mechanisms for local interactions is paramount, in order to instil a sense of professionalism.

2. **Professionalism:** While local interactions privilege the interactions of local people who are directly concerned, professionalism here pays attention to what is/should be at the centre of those interactions and how the interactions unfold. The diary extract below illustrates the point.

I think that the DRC education system needs better teachers and primary/secondary school leaders. So a programme that touches on pedagogical and leadership theories and practices is important. However, a three, four or five year long programme needs further topics from areas related to teaching and leadership. I found philosophy interesting during my university studies, but (behavioural, developmental and social) psychology

100

is also important for understanding children. There is however another factor: that of the DRC being a post-war country and counselling/psychology might be more useful for teachers to deal with whatever trauma that might be out there than philosophy or sociology

Questioning any given body of knowledge, defining the depth and breadth of formal knowledge (Freidson 2001) while recognising its tacit dimension are what might come out of professionalisation that is done within the context of local interactions. The downside to the above extract is that, although it takes context from prior (local) interactions into account, it does not explicitly involve an input from other individuals, which would have given professionalism a collaborative mode (Whitty 2008). There will always be practical constraints for building collaborative networks/mechanisms. Coupled with humans' innate ability to develop ideas anywhere, this means that (intense) training (Hargreaves 2003), as a way of updating others on recent developments in a particular field, may define professional work at universities.

Other forms of professionalism such as the traditional, managerial, collaborative and democratic modes have their strengths and limitations, at least in settings such as the United Kingdom (Whitty 2008). That is why sensitivity to local interactions becomes essential in determining the dominant approach to professionalism. The suggestion here, therefore, is for curriculum design and conduct of affairs in the DRC universities to be done while recognising local interactions and (international and local) context-relevant knowledge systems. This is more likely to produce relevant programmes leading to "devotion to a transcendent value which infuses its specialisation with a large and putatively higher goal ..." (Freidson 2001:122). As argued earlier, the aim here is not to make of the DRC universities places where one learns *anything* or *everything*. In the context of scarce resources felt more so in places that are already experiencing hardship like the DRC and Sub-Saharan Africa, focused and clearly defined higher education *teaching that breaks*

101

the limits in learning is essential. What is meant by *teaching that breaks the limits of learning* is linked to the next key element.

3. **Lifelong education:** It was suggested earlier that learning should take a lifelong character rather than be limited to university lecture rooms. In some literature "lifelong learning" is an essential tenet where individuals can no longer be satisfied with gained membership to a professional body but endeavour to constantly update their professional knowledge (Guile and Lucas 1999). In the context of curriculum design and direction of higher education in the DRC and Sub-Saharan Africa, a nuanced understanding of 'lifelong education' is necessary. Below is a diary extract that I use as a metaphor to illustrate this point.

Many students studying at DRC universities have told me that they sometimes sit on windows and even outside lecture theatres to follow their lectures. If this has been a funding and/or management problem that might take time to resolve, then a lesson needs to be learnt and perhaps use this example as a metaphor for learning being drawn out of the established learning grounds into the world and life.

It could be argued from the above extract that teaching should be tailored and programmes designed in such a way that learning is more focused on the acquisition of lifelong skills. Expert knowledge still matters but the skills to assess situations and absorb/analyse new knowledge become essential methodological learning aspects of lifelong education. Bolstering incremental subject, cultural etc. knowledge may be the by-product of such an approach to learning at higher education level.

However, with the rise of terrorism and especially the breakdown of trust between subject and agency as demonstrated in Chapter 2, university curriculum design has a unique responsibility. That responsibility/challenge is best exemplified in developing people's lifelong ability to assess the strengths and limitations of their stances toward the knowledge to be derived from both life's critical incidents (Cunningham 2008) and everyday occurrences is more likely to lead to both technologically and economically skilled people (Giddens 1984) able to transform living standards, as well as mature generations who can stand the pressures of possible religious and cultural fundamentalism.

Adopting methodological inquiry in a wholesale manner is less preferred to enabling different indigenous approaches and innovation to emerge (Denzin and Lincoln 2008; Sikes 2006). This is not to say that external concepts and approaches cannot find their way in the DRC or Sub-Saharan universities. Instead, as I argue, more extensively in the previous chapter looking specifically at "de-contextualisation", those being introduced to arguably "foreign" theories, practices and methodologies should be able to articulate how and why they are using them.

4. Quality assurance: All aspects of this proposed framework are interlinked and to some extent local interactions, professionalism and lifelong education add to the quality of a programme of study and direction of a university/higher education institute. However, as a formal process, effective internal quality assurance that seems to be having a positive effect in some universities (Beso et al. 2008) is partly what is going to restore credibility in universities in the DRC and Sub-Saharan Africa. Review board meetings, external examiners/verifiers, second markers, reviews, standardisations, professional associations, licencing/awarding bodies and resource centres are just some examples of ensuring what Giddens calls institutional reflexivity, such that there are regular processes of loss and re-appropriation of everyday skills and knowledge (Beck et al. 1994). However, any institutional quality assurance reflexivity needs to be holistic, meaning inclusive of internal as well as external factors.

One can argue that an insular/closed educational institution is a thing of the past. The brain-drain challenge that African higher education faces (Teferra and Albatch 2004) is just one example to illustrate the idea that higher education institutes are systems that interact and are interdependent with the external environment. Any internal processes of conforming to standards and continuous improvement can be compromised by external factors and the DRC and the Sub-Saharan Africa have their specific ones that need to be understood and anticipated. Here are some examples that may compromise quality:

The proliferation of private universities in the DRC and perhaps elsewhere in Sub Saharan Africa is an indication of the attraction that this sector represents in educating the masses. However, the fight for institutional survival/competition can result in the dampening down of standards to keep student enrolment figures up.

Everyone has their own image of a teacher or university lecturers. Here, a teacher/lecture is not viewed as a ruler who "is free to do good turns for his subordinates, in return for gifts or dues" (Beck et al 1994:83). The following diary extract gives some background thinking behind this positioning.

The Unesco's 2010 report suggests that there are not enough academic and scientific staff in the DRC's higher education institutions. However, the few that are there have various other commitments. Some combine teaching with high profile posts in state institutions, various cabinet jobs and commitment to political parties. A student in one of the DRC's universities once told me that he saw his professor once and for the rest of the year they had to make do with his assistants. Despite a student's best effort, you must buy teacher's notes and the assistant's practice notes if you want to stand any chance of success.

And the following from a concerned parent whose child attends a higher education institute in Cameroon:

> My daughter asks me for money to pay for her university fees and everything. But it seems like the quality of university teaching is purposefully sub-standard to force students to pay for extra, more serious and rigorous teaching sessions run privately by the same university teachers. It's like a parallel system.

Diminishing standards of living seem to have led to a trend where there is a constant demand for students to support staff financially which reverses normal practice of staff supporting students in lifelong skills and knowledge acquisition. Another factor to consider from the above extract is that the institutional quality of any given higher education institute could badly be damaged by individual staff's success stories in the wider local environment that is competing with universities for ownership of expertise. While working to promote the kind of commitment that goes beyond the call of duty and discuss, through local interactions, professional ethical issues (Lunt 2008), it is important to consider the external needs of employees to preserve quality. Perry et al. (2006) is just an example in a plethora of literature on the theories of motivation. However, it is both the responsibility of universities and national leaders to work collaboratively in order to ensure that the wider environment does not diminish but instead improves the quality of higher education institutes.

The need for financial support to maintain quality in terms of paying staff a fair wage, for example, can mean creating and maintaining financial ties with private parties whose interests could relegate the impartiality of coded knowledge (Beck et al. 1994). The politicisation/spiritualisation of university posts can also compromise autonomy and the impartiality of science.

Conclusion

The main objective of this chapter was to reflect on what is involved in producing and sustaining a relevant programme of study for higher education/universities in the DRC and Sub-Saharan Africa. In so doing, the argument led to the setting of an agenda for the direction/leadership that such institutions need to take as they negotiate their own paths to success. The analysis has highlighted that excellence can be achieved through local interactions, professionalism, lifelong education and quality assurance.

Despite my best effort in translating (from French to English) the objectives that higher education institutions are set in the DRC, it still remains a human effort with imperfections that could affect the accuracy of conclusions drawn in relation to their strengths and limitations. The lack of clearly defined guidelines from the DRC's higher institutions on what is involved in the formulation of a programme of study is also a weakness, not only of this chapter but also of any university that has to operate in an environment with little or no guidelines on essential questions discussed here. Nevertheless, this hopefully coherent framework for action can be critiqued, enriched and used to support current and future adaptation, transformation, reformation and revitalisation work (Amoono-Neizer 1998) in the DRC and Sub-Saharan Africa.

It has been argued in the first chapter that "a cross-field engagement with social phenomenon that is constructed through the interplay of structure and agency is what is needed" in the exercise of African leadership. Higher education being one of those fields, this framework (especially the first two tenets) therefore represents an overt way of embodying a healthy relationship between structure (universities) and agency (individuals that are, at least, directly concerned with their university's curriculum and future direction).

Acknowledgement:
I am grateful to Christopher Boxall for his critical readership and proofreading an earlier version of this chapter.

Chapter 6

Body sociology and Africa

Introduction

Following on from the publication of the first edition, more questions have arisen. The publication somewhat exonerated the African Ubuntu-based philosophy or sociology as the source of the problems and, instead, placed it as the solution to leadership problems in Africa. It seems unnecessary to rehearse the arguments that have now been tightened up and I would refer the reader to previous chapters to familiarise oneself with the perspective. The first edition, to put it plainly, has shown that there is nothing wrong with the African conception of social reality that, if followed in the way I demonstrate here, should lead to better leadership practices where interdependent force-beings (agents and structures) collaboratively shape a better future within the framework of decreased fear and increased self-scrutiny.

It could be argued, however, that previous chapters approach the subject from an entirely cognitive sociological perspective. By this I mean to say that, in the discussions about Ubuntu and structuration theory, 'human agency became equated with consciousness and the mind, rather than the management of the body as a whole' (Shilling 2008:8-9). The cynic, therefore, would be quick to point out that the underexplored body sociology could provide some clues to the problems. It is incorrect to think that the body was not talked about at all but, perhaps, not clearly enough and to that extent the body sociology took on an 'absent presence' (ibid.) in the discussions.

The cynic, however, determined to find something intrinsically wrong with the very existence of an African could point to this inadequately examined realm of being human to respond 'yes' to the question 'do Africans have rotten bodies that corrupt their cognition, hence the endemic corruption, human rights abuses and stubborn poverty levels?' I should point out that no one sets out to prove such a supposition. It would be counterproductive to the advancement of humankind to make such a prejudiced aim the focus of one's study. At the same time, well informed and rigorous analysis is warranted to counter conspiracy theorists in a world where anybody, at the touch of a button, can feed into a complex flow of information.

This chapter starts off with a brief outline of the wider literature on body sociology. In an attempt to broaden the scope of my analysis, I will respond to the cynic at this early stage. This will allow me briefly to survey some specific African literature, to understand how the African body in its active (living) and inactive (dead) form is regarded/treated. Bracketing what the cynic thinks about the African body, I will draw on Chapter Seven's analysis to outline how Africans have approached the body within the FS model.

Insight into the body sociology: a snapshot of the wider literature

Despite the field receiving limited attention in classical sociology, Shilling (2008) notes a resurgent interest in body sociology in the 1980s. The explosion of interest in the body has taken many forms, ranging from gendered bodies, reproductive bodies, children's bodies, disabled bodies, racialised bodies, digitised bodies and aging bodies to name but a few. Shilling (1993), however, identifies four main reasons or developments that would account for a renewed interest in the body in sociology: consumerism, demographic changes with concerns surrounding health and the body, feminist critiques, and body technologies that have given rise to implants and virtual existence. Useful as it is, Shilling's categorisation should be viewed as open to further enrichment. I would argue that given the historical magnitude of the slave trade and colonisation, the hard fought independence of African nations should not be viewed simply as an exercise of handing over territorial control. It is a continuous decolonising celebration of the African body. Hence, race should be viewed at the same level as gender and black/racialised sociology, placed alongside feminist critiques.

I do not have limitless space to engage in a detailed discussion about how consumerism, demographic changes, feminist critiques, body technologies, and now racialised bodies, have been conceptualised in international literature. I will, therefore, be very selective from the above list and discuss racialised bodies only in the context of their historical significance on the African continent. That said, racialised bodies have been marked by major historical moments that would seem to either positively characterise a given race as perfect, while negatively debasing others as diseased entities, either to be destroyed, healed, humanised and/or civilised. Racial and bodily impurities are what the cynic, as illustrated in the introduction, would base his or her unscientific argument on in order to engineer some form of ethnic cleansing or colonising enterprise.

Dr Edgar Schulz did just that in 1935, when he tried to demonstrate that 'high rates of insanity (manic depression and dementia praecox), feeble-mindedness, hysteria, and suicide ...arose from the fact that Jews were not, strictly speaking, a single race, but rather an amalgamation of Negro and Oriental blood' (Proctor 2008, 93). Ultimately, gas chambers were seen as a more effective way of dealing with the issue than sterilisation. The idea of humanistic colonisation (Cooper 2006) took a rather developmental/evolutionary approach, even though such a view cannot be used to justify well documented human cruelty for egotistical motives. The point, nevertheless, is that the body as a race has been held as either perfect or impure and as an undeveloped physical and metaphysical entity.

109

When seeking to discuss African bodies, then, the link between the physical entity that we can see and the immaterial self is almost inherent, to the point that an attack on race implies an attack on the person's very self. This racial caricaturing has no scientific basis and, as eloquently argued in Fullwiley's (2015:37) summary of the latest scientific report: the Human Genome Project (HGP), she confidently disavows that racial differences had a genetic basis from the first highly publicised unveiling of the Human Genome Draft Map in 2000. This only confirms the long-standing struggle against racism that, for many, is a repulsively dehumanising and unethical phenomenon, manifesting itself through segregation, antisemitism, slavery and colonisation.

Initially, the struggle to emancipate yesterday's victims of racism did take on the trend of awakening the world to see beyond the body. But holding such a position is also problematic, as it fails to account for the totality of the person. The obsession with race in a negative way and the drive to see beyond race (the physical body) only highlights an unnecessary dualism. Cheville's (2005) concern for compounding even further the body and mind dichotomy pushed her to propose 'embodied cognition' as a theoretical framework that reconciles cognitive and body sociologies. The body is perceived here as interface of cultural cognition and, at the same time, the body 'exerts subjective influence on the mind' (91). Such a link, it would appear, was already advocated by Foucault, whose study of prisons brought him to argue that modern prisons seek to instil in the mind a state of constant visibility, by subjecting the body to permanent surveillance through the use of lights in panopticon architecture (Bartkey 2008). Shilling (2001:341) is also of the view that the body sociology should be about 'the corporal character of social life'. In the following section, I explore the corporality of African social life by referring to the works of authors, such as Axel (1998), Cadwel et al. (1997), Cohen and Odhiambo (1992), Letsheke (2013) and Smaje (1997).

Insight into the body sociology: African/Afrocentric literature

The renewed interest in the body in the 1980s (Shilling 2008), one or two decades after European colonial domination, is at the very least a reversal of an imperialist narrative that characterised the black man as emotional, highly embodied, especially sexually, and therefore infantile compared to the white man (Lupton 1998). That said, what the concept of the African body evokes in the minds and feelings of the colonised is underexplored.

Emerging from a history of domination, justice is therefore fundamental in conceptualising (African) race/body. Philosophically, justice is a concept of reason with no direct object of experience (Curtis 2006). Historically, however, the aspiration for 'a racially just society' presupposes a time and space that have been dominated by discrimination and bias towards a particular race and have required emancipatory actions to make the world a more equal place.

Smaje (1997:307-8) would perhaps argue that texts such as *Feared and Revered: Media Representations of the Racialised and Gendered Bodies-A Case Study* (Neal 2008) and *Gendered and Racial Violence and Spatialised Justice: The Murder of Pamela George* (Razack 2008) are 'empirical studies which demonstrate the discrimination and disadvantage experienced by people from racial or ethnic minorities…to postulate categories of material exclusion…' Smaje, however, argues that such an approach backgrounds other important issues of the *meaning* of race, upon which *relational* social constructs (material exclusion, for example) of race are based. Smaje's (1997) analytical project highlights the meaning of being black as a biological state of being, with a corresponding black ontology beyond the functional social categorisations.

Smaje's perspective is quite unique in that it frames the African body beyond the reactionary approach of racial

111

emancipatory advocacy. However, what Smaje and other African body/race sociologists do not do is conceptualise trends in the way that the African body is regarded/treated within an 'exclusively' African context. Such an approach is more than imperative, in order to grasp African realities and interrogate certain African practices with regard to the body. I attempt to do that within the vocation of humanisation, structuration theory, otherwise known here as (Ubu)*ntu* ontology. Up to now, I perceive the field of the 'African body' to be disjointed, despite the variety of theorising that I discuss below under specific themes, such as culturally embodied, tortured, impure, rainbowed and faceless bodies.

Africans are *culturally embodied* and there are several examples to point to that being the case. Without intending to make this a place or moment to pass judgement on various cultural practices, male and female circumcision is one such example. 'For both sexes, the genital operation is essential in becoming a fully adult member of society (Caldwell et al. 1997, 1186 citing Myers et al. 1985:587).

Cultured bodies are not necessarily communal bodies. By that, I mean the physical body may embody the African culture but it is realistically impossible to have a communal body, since the body is by nature one/singular. This, however, does not prevent Africans from using a singular body to impact on wider culture. The *tortured bodies* in the African context can include all those from privileged and non-privileged backgrounds who (seem to) give out contradictory beliefs and cognitions to the official (cultural and state) ones. Examples of this are the beating, torturing and forced imprisonment of opposition and human rights activists in some places. They may also include all those who, in the process of overcoming contradictory beliefs and cognitions, are either systematically or collaterally tortured. It is possible to view the countless rape cases in Eastern DRC in this light.

Africans also perceive of the body as *pure or impure, sick or healthy,* although the contrasting concepts are not exclusive to

112

Africa. Meditation in Buddhism is understood to be a powerful tool to bring believers to the realisation of the impermanence of the bodily nature of the world. That impermanence has, however, been conveyed, especially in medieval Japan, through the impurity and foulness of the human body in general and the female body in particular (Pandey 2005). With or without the religious overtones, all or some bodies in Africa are portrayed as impure, sick, while others are treated as pure and healthy. In the case of exorcism, some of these impure bodies are ritualised (by willing/fearless agents and low scrutinised pastors) into becoming pure. Some of those regarded as possessing 'impure' bodies are simply mistreated by other agents under the gaze of disinterested, ineffective and perhaps conniving institutions. As already discussed in Chapter 1, Letseke's (2013) accounts of incidents of indiscretions against gay, albino and disabled people across the continent, attest to pure and impure characterisations of the African body by Africans. There are several reasons advanced for such impurity of learners with disability, and the same could be said about the above groups of people. Eskay et al.'s (2012, 478) survey of the literature returned the following reasons:

A cure from God (due to gross disobedience to God's commandments; ancestral violation of societal norms (e.g., due to stealing); offences against gods of the land (e.g., fighting within society); breaking laws and family sins (e.g., stealing and denying); misfortune (e.g., due to marriage incest); witches and wizards (e.g., society saw them as witches and wizards); adultery (a major abomination); a warning from the gods of the land (due to pollution of water and the land); arguing and fighting with the elders (a societal taboo); misdeed in the previous life (such as stealing); illegal and unapproved marriage by the societal elders (arguing and fighting against elderly advice in marriage); possession by evil spirits (due to gross societal disobedience); and many others.

The authors go on to call it an African education; that which Nigerians enjoyed prior to colonisation, where able and disabled

113

bodies mixed indiscriminately. In my view, a fair analysis needs to consider Africa's own (culturally) entrenched sense of bodily impurities that need to be critiqued further in order to develop an ontological understanding of how, where and when an African body is valued or disvalued within the framework of Ubuntu.

I will use two pieces of literatures, one looking at a case in Kenya and the other focused on South Africa, to advance a further contrasting category: the *faceless* and *rainbowed* bodies. Cohen and Odhiambo (1992) describe the legal case in Kenya following the death of a famous Luo tribe lawyer SM Otieno, who was married to a Kikuyu (another tribe) lady. Having been buried in the Kenyan capital (Nairobi) according to the wishes of the widow, the relatives of SM Otieno fought through the courts to win a reburial in their homeland according to traditional law. What this literature also highlights, according to Cohen and Odhiambo, is how questions begin to be raised about ordinary disadvantaged people, who are discounted until a prominent case involving prominent people, like that of *SM Otieno*, comes up; then these faceless bodies, called *raia*, begin to matter.

While some bodies matter more than others, as highlighted above, the diversity of African bodies are instead celebrated as a colourful rainbow to be proud of in other places. The concept of 'Rainbowed' bodies, in contrast, comes from the 'body politics' where, in an effort to overcome racial domination in the case of South Africa for example, the subject of any colour is a subject for the whole society. Though this view is somewhat challenged in 'the possibility that the body is not so much a pre-given vessel in which the nation may reside, but, rather, has been constituted historically and dialectically in relation to processes of colonialism, capitalism and nation-form' (Axel 1998:16), the discourse of building a 'rainbow nation' itself is indicative of the maturity of a people wrestling with body inequalities that push others to become faceless.

114

Related to *cultured bodies*, one could argue for another category called *ritualised bodies* that communities or individuals use to, 1) make a point about an issue that is important to them, 2) celebrate or show happiness about the whole or an aspect of bodies, and 3) mark an important aspect of a communal culture. The young man burning his body in Tunisia to make a point about an aspect of social life that he was unhappy with, resulting in what is commonly known as the Arab spring, and some women in Kenya protesting naked - again to highlight social injustices. These are some examples for reason (1) of the ritualised bodies category. Celebrations of black pride across the world and in parts of Africa are examples of reason (2), and the famous trial documented in *Burying SM* (Cohen and Odhiambo 1992), highlights the particular attention that Africans give to inanimate (dead) bodies.

There are clearly broad perspectives of body sociology in Africa and the categories identified are part of by no means an exhaustive list. Some of them evoke negative and/or positive emotions. Negative trends, you could argue, are those examples including slavery, racism, apartheid, black on black racism, ill treatment of minority races, female mutilation, and the Rwandan genocide. The positive ones could include black artists and high profile religious and political figures leading to pride in the African body and the many other cases mentioned above.

I am of the view that most of the above categories are descriptive rather than explanatory. They offer some useful classifications, without necessarily explaining to us why those who are *faceless* in one African context would be considered as 'rainbowed' bodies in another African context. It does not explain why you are likely to find mass graves in one place, while one person's funeral in another place would draw thousands to come and pay their respects.

An explanatory analysis, which enables us not only to understand but also endeavour to promote what is perceived as positive and change what is seen as negative is therefore required. To do that, a grasp of the fundamentals of a people's

115

ontological and methodological approaches, enabling us to explain the different manifestations of how the African body is treated by Africans, is essential. In the interest of clarity, my advice, that you may choose to heed or not, is to read Chapter 7 first, in which I outline the FS methodology of structuration that will, I hope, make it easier to follow the next section of this chapter.

Reframing African body sociology: a preliminary exercise

Beyond the aforementioned negative and positive sentiments, the cognition that is embodied in the African body must be thought of first and foremost as going through a relational existence that promotes and/or diminishes the (African) body's role in the shaping and reshaping of its institutions. I will regroup the above 'descriptive' categories of the African body under four explanatory scenarios that are consistent with the methodology of structuration I outline in the next chapter.

Scenario 1: Let us consider the example of cultured bodies, where boys and girls, for whom culture has become so pervasive, that they willingly put themselves through a genital operation at the hands of a leading traditional surgeon (whose blades may or may not be sterilised). There are also examples where patients who believe or are made to believe that their bodies are possessed are consensually brought to a leading pastor, who later prescribes a private consultation where the body is either trampled upon or sexually exploited. Similarly, Madzokere and Machingura (2015) investigate false prophets/esses, using evidence from Zimbabwe, who prey on believers desperate for miracles, including one's body being healed. There is also a 'body count' trend where 'willing and fearless' partaking bodies in board meetings, regional and national assemblies/dialogues assemble and, once the quorum is reached, the institutions begin to scheme in an effort to turn their unscrutinised agendas into reality (see case study 4 in Chapter 7). In this case, the African body is wrapped in an ontological bubble where the agent is low in fear, while the leader of the institution enjoys low self-scrutiny. (Low fear agents and low self-scrutinising institutions, Q1 see Chapter 7).

Scenario 2: Now let us turn to impure, tortured and faceless bodies and ask ourselves, how do we, as part of the human race, reach this point? It is often the case that the 'impure' bodies of albinos, tortured political and human rights activists and the faceless masses do not consensually agree to their bodies being treated in such a way. On the contrary, these agents are living in high fear, even though some manage to break through the obscured agency to assert themselves and their beliefs. This high fear that the African body endures is contrasted by (can be met with) low self-scrutinising institutions. In such a cases, the institutions tend to be in denial of any wrongdoing with no intention or urgency to carry out investigations. Such a treatment of the African body is not surprising in an environment, where the sacredness of an African body is not decided by a 'God', as might be claimed by those trying to use God's name deceptively to carry out their dubious acts, like in scenario 1; what is sacred and worth respecting, or spending money on the autopsies of tortured bodies, is up to the leader. (High fear agents and low self-scrutinising institutions, Q2 see Chapter 7).

Scenario 3: Keeping the above scenario in mind, imagine now that the institution is beginning to scrutinise itself more, not because it wants to show respect to the African body but to justify its impure, tortured and faceless condition. 'The police was acting in self-defence' is often used to justify brutality; 'we do not have a law in place to bury *les indigènes* (the indigenous)' was an explanation advanced by some authorities at the discovery of 'institution-sponsored' mass graves; and 'the country is outraged that the wrong people are being tried to protect the real culprits'. These are some of the statements you might hear from different constituencies in Africa, which suggests an ontological mind-set in which the African (tortured, impure and faceless) body is charged with high fear, while the
117

institutions are in some form of high self-scrutiny that only seeks to justify the ill-treatment of the African body. (High fear for agents and high 'self-scrutiny' for institutions, Q3 see Chapter 7)

Scenario 4: The *ntu* (or Ubuntu) way of conceptualising the African body is in my view the vocation of the African body. I would now invite the reader to reconsider the categories of rainbowed and ritualised bodies given in the previous section. Questions might be raised as to whether a singular body could be a vessel in which the nation resides (Axel 1998). However, the palpable signs of a South African society where people are increasingly in tune with the idea that the country's space is a theatre for equal rights for multi-coloured bodies is testament to low fear that was once shown during the years of struggle against apartheid, which has resulted in high scrutinising institutions.

In this fourth scenario, there is a sense of increased independent research, which may reveal perhaps contradictory, unknown facts about the African body. Gitau et al. (2014), for example, have found that their sample of black South African adolescents were more favourable to their overweight silhouettes than their white counterparts. Another non-definitive study by Mwaba and Roman (2009) has found, in some black South African female students, a low level of dissatisfaction with their bodies. This, however, may not be the case in other places or with the same people in other times, as globalisation impacts on people's perceptions about their (African) bodies.

In extreme cases, the African body has agentically been used with low fear to force institutions into becoming more self-scrutinising. The poignant case of the Tunisian man burning himself, which sparked off what is commonly referred to as the 'Arab Spring', is one such example. If all the man was interested in was maximising the number of human deaths, it is possible to imagine him embarking on the indiscriminate killing of whoever and whatever crossed his path. Instead, he instantly or with some premeditation, took his own life by burning his own (African) body. While not encouraging suicide, it does highlight how

118

indiscriminate killing (through terrorist acts) is a cowardly and hollow exercise of destroying just about 'any' body, in order to advance an ideology. There is, in fact, no link between the body and an ideology other than the fear the perpetrators of such actions seek to create. In the case of the Tunisian man burning his body, or the topless East Nigerian women in 1929, exposing their bodies to protest against an issue of significance to them, the African body here is displaying extreme and absolute low fear, intent on forcing institutions to show equally (extreme and) absolute and extreme self-scrutiny.

Were these Africans taking a risk? The answer to that question could be 'No' if you are approaching the matter from an entirely cognitive sociological point of view. According to Giddens' (2002:22) 'the notion of risk, (…), is inseparable from the ideas of probability and uncertainty. A person cannot be said to be running a risk where an outcome is 100 percent certain'. To prove his point, Giddens uses the analogy of a person who decides to jump off a skyscraper and reassures him/herself that things are thus far fine each time he passes a floor on his way to the inevitable outcome, 'death'. Let us now suppose that the person wasn't reassuring him/herself at all. Instead, s/he was rather saying 'I'm fed up with this, I hope my death changes something'. Then we begin to notice that the (black) body is the corporal interface of his/her social life (Shilling, opcit). The inevitability of death and the most intimate exposure of (female) body parts being the immediate outcome, as illustrated in the above examples, does not diminish the uncertainty of the social risk being taken to change institutions for the better.

The non-ntu ill practices are notoriously too stubborn to let institutions serve the needs of all and, alone, these shocking individual/group acts, as illustrated above, do not put an automatic end to them, however powerful and necessary they are. They may trigger increased scrutiny for a brief period of time but (only) sustained low fear agentic actions will ensure that institutions continue to remain highly self-scrutinising. Such actions will need mediation by and appreciation of all African bodies.

Not only would one criticise Giddens for focussing his analysis on a cognitive social perspective, he, I think, was also mistaken to suggest that risk is not a characteristic of traditional societies but of modern industrial civilisation (the West in other words). The reason for that, according to Giddens, is the assumption, that unlike modern industrial societies, traditional societies are not future-oriented in terms of wanting to conquer it. The distant unknown future that needs to be conquered and controlled, in my view, is not only about seeking to see beyond where one's eyes cannot in time but also gaining a lateral view of the blind spots about where things are and should be today and in times to come. Conquering the future is about uncovering blind spots, and Giddens' approach seems to have focused entirely on the blind spots moving forward, forgetting that there are lateral blind spots. The protesting Nigerian women could arguably be located in African traditional societies but with a lateral social approach to the future.

The famous *Burying SM* (Cohen and Odhiambo 1992), if happening both for the privileged and *faceless* raia, would be another manifestation of how the African body, even in its inanimate state, continues to be a subject of freedom, reverence and respect within a context of transparent legal and cultural institutions. For some, this case highlighted just how much the Luo and Kikuyu tribes were entrenched in their tribal logic to the detriment of national cohesion. What the above authors also argue is that both sides had Luo witnesses to support their side of the argument which, points to the issue being much more than a tribal case, a point missed even by foreign reporters. On the contrary, Cohen and Odhiambo (ibid: 76) describe the whole case as "having the potential of revealing much about the various 'republics of free discourse' within the 'Luo nation'". I would argue that this is rather a vivid example of how the African body should be treated within an *ntu* perspective, where low fear

120

agents are able to take a case up and expect institutions to act with high self-scrutiny (transparency).

Conclusion

I want to end this chapter by arguing that this exclusively African conceptual framing of the African body has the potential to serve as the basis to reconsider previous literatures and guide future discussions on the subject of the African body. For illustrative purposes, let us briefly look at Bates' (2007) article, which explores various representations of the African body with HIV. The author uses posters and photographs to argue that the African (HIV infected) body is wrapped around two narratives. One narrative, which is reminiscent of colonial rhetoric, portrays the African body to an outside audience (mainly UK) as dirty and degenerate, while the other narrative (aimed at the South African audience) shows the African (HIV infected) body as empowered. It is easy to criticise such representations on the grounds that they are only crafted with the purpose of persuading a wealthy audience to donate money to a particular cause.

On the subject of body scarification in Africa, Torres De Souza and Agostini (2012:105) write

The reasons these marks were adopted could vary significantly. As ethnographic studies carried out in different African regions have indicated, they could be used for beautification (Adepegba 1976:39; Bohannan 1987; David et al. 1988:370; Drewal 1989:247), for indication of health or social status (Adepegba 1976:29–30), for indicating life-cycle stage (Berns 2000:262–265), for initiatory rituals (Schneider 1973:26; Lincoln 1975:325; Robert 1987:46; Berns 2000:262), for medicinal purposes (David et al. 1988:370; Drewal 1989:245; Ojo 2008:367), for distinguishing ethnicity (Law 1997:205; Ojo 2008:367), as a sign of sorrow (Drewal 1987:83), for sexual pleasure (Lima 1956; Adepegba 1976:39), and as a sign of civilization (Vogel 1998:99).

121

What this chapter has done is to advance four conceptual narratives (scenarios) that can be used to ground the above studies, as well as Bates' two narratives. The narrative of HIV infected Africans being portrayed to a UK audience as diseased can be analysed further to understand whether it fits into scenario 1, 2 or 3. As for the empowered HIV infected African body, this conceptualisation is firmly rooted in scenario 4, which, while recognising the need for HIV medical treatment, values the African body as an empowered agent able to shape and reshape his/her structures. It is, therefore, not a misrepresentation to use scenario 1, 2 and 3 narratives to advance scenario 4's agenda. Bates describes this agenda to be an 'empowered African body', which could mean a strong, active and healthy body (despite the infection in this case) able to shape its social reality. On the subjects of *health* and *economic growth*, research shows a strong link between the two (Bloom et al. 2004), which makes it possible to argue that one's economic capital equals the health capital of agents, whose productivity depends on the nature of their fear and self-scrutiny within a methodological structuration of a given environment. Hence, the equation below:

Economic capital

$$= \frac{\text{Health (body) Capital of agents}}{\text{FS Methodology of Structuration (ntu ontology) of a particular field}}$$
$$(Q1,2,3,4 \text{ giving Sceanios } 1,2,3,4)$$

The above equation can serve as a source for further research, in as much as I would recommend further research, especially in the artistic expressions of the African body through paintings, sculptures, music etc. In addition to the gigantic statues erected at major roundabouts of African cities or the compulsory portrait of a country's leader that only portray the institutional narrative about both the body and cognitive social reality of a people, more attention needs to be paid to how the

African body, in art and written policy, is represented in fields such as hospitals, schools, and other institutions.

Chapter 7

The FS (Fear and Self-Scrutiny) methodology of Ubuntu: a mapping of the field

Introduction:

This chapter is both summative and elaborative. It summarises the entire enterprise from first to second edition and it elaborates, for the first time, what I call the 'FS (Fear and self-scrutiny) methodology of Ubuntu or structuration'.

Let us agree that *Africa through Structuration theory – ntu* has been successful in demonstrating, not only *where* things should be in terms of African leadership whether political or in other fields, but also *how* we should go about them. However, it is still unclear *where* African leadership practices are right now. Hence the question: How far removed from or close to the proposed leadership ideals are current African leadership practices?

This final chapter essentially answers the above question. While I attempt to characterise certain leadership practices, the reader needs to be reminded that the intention is not to pigeonhole leaders or nations. It is quite possible that a leader, who is overwhelmingly of a particular quadrant, could display some traits associated with another quadrant, as shall be illustrated especially with approaches to traditions. However, the model that is based on several examples from various African countries is a guide that citizens can use to get an idea of how close or far removed they are from the ultimate quadrant (*ntu* leadership). Each quadrant will carry a symbolic name; it will have a leading question, as typically asked by the type of leader associated with that quadrant, and frame how tradition, knowledge, education, legality, legitimacy, fear and self-scrutiny are conceptualised.

The chapter starts with a brief mapping of leadership theorising and practice in Africa so far. This is followed by definitions of the terms of reference before engaging in a step-by-step discussion of each quadrant. As well as using the FS methodology of structuration to understand tribalism, the analysis also seeks to define the guiding ethical principles of each quadrant. It goes on to discuss patterns of movement within the model and evaluates the effectiveness of existing systems designed to enable movement towards Ubuntu leadership, before making a case for the way ahead. The chapter ends with what is termed here as the *Singapore conundrum*.

A brief mapping of the field

It is the case that the FS methodology of structuration is a different conceptualisation from existing published literature. However, an attempt to refer to other bodies of knowledge and perhaps point out some similarities and differences is necessary for the continuity and discontinuity of the overall discourse.

With the intensification of scholarly work since the end of colonisation, Zoogah and Nkomo's (2013) adapted figure below offers a credible framework within which to conceptualise research and management practices in Africa.

High	Territorial	Instrumental
Different from West		
Low	Symbolic	Sentimental

Low   Similar to West   High

Territorial research and management/leadership seek to advance a uniquely African stance that is very different from the West. The symbolic one is not concerned with a unique approach and emphasises neither African nor Western/global identities. The sentimental approach seeks to underline the similarities and at the same time overlook the differences. Instrumental, or what I would prefer to call comparative and recommended by the above authors, seeks to define both the differences and similarities in research and leadership practices in Africa and outside of it.

I would argue that, for the sake of the advancement of unbiased research, the above four areas of research on leadership and management practices can only be adopted as an initial research intention that does not seek to massage the data in order to accomplish some predetermined ends. It is therefore possible, as demonstrated in earlier chapters, that one can analyse Ubuntu from a territorial stance and end up with an instrumental/comparative outcome. I also looked at leadership from an instrumental/comparative view (by using structuration theory), which led to affirming a territorial African ontological/leadership identity. The FS methodology of Ubuntu (structuration), therefore, stems from a dynamic conceptualisation that moves from territorial to comparative and vice versa.

Whatever the starting point, I will briefly discuss some trends, with particular regard to political governance in Africa. In *Constitutional Democracy in Africa*, Nwabueze (1984) profiles a positive trend in Africa as more and more nations begin to build their state structures around a set of constitutional principles that would guarantee greater justice, peace, stability and development. In as much as Ben Nwabueze's points are valid, they do not tell the full story. I shall demonstrate later that even democratic, autocratic systems or whatever name is given to particular ways of governing, have their own constitutions and set of constitutionalists. Constitutional democracies, therefore, need to be seen within a bigger picture.

Some blame Africa's misfortune either on the colonial arbitrary imposition of states or on current African leadership (Miti et al. 2010). I regard the first reason as a red herring, implying that Africans are incapable of resolving a clearly fixable problem through *ntu* leadership. Outside of *ntu* or Ubuntu, on which I base my argument/model, others have characterised leadership in Africa in terms of good and bad governance. Drawing from other sources, Akokpari (2010) characterises good governance as displaying impartial rules/laws, policies conducive to economic growth and democratic institutions. In the preponderantly bad governance category, the author lists some salient features, such as: one party dominance, corruption, politicisation of ethnicity or tribalism, and poverty, among others. The author goes on to highlight the important role of regional bodies, especially the New Partnership for Africa's Development (Nepad) in helping those countries with bad governance to improve.

John Akokpari concludes with a little dose of honesty, pointing to the difficulty of characterising African political culture or leadership/governance. Hence there is the tendency, in my view, to provide a descriptive leadership narrative instead of a theorised explanatory analysis based on certain descriptions. For example, why are there impartial laws? How does tribalism manifest itself? Why do some one-party state systems succeed to impose themselves and others fail? These are just a few of the questions that point to the need for much deeper reflection, not only to put our finger on the fundamental characteristics of various forms of governance in Africa but also explain how they can come about. To do that, as I argued in the first edition, one has to view governance as depended on how social reality in a particular setting is formed. Either from the angle of Giddens' structuration theory or Africa's Ubuntu, I have demonstrated that social reality in Africa is based on an interdependence of force-beings (not only between individuals but also between the subjects and institutions they create). I posited that *Fear* and *self-scrutiny* are two key indicators. I will now further explain how it works, so as to give the reader a sense of an overall descriptive and explanatory mapping grounded on an African ontology (Ubuntu) and also structuration theory that has now resulted in what I call the FS methodology of *ntu*/structuration.

Terms of reference

There are several key concepts that can be discussed here. Freedom House defines a free country as one that has open political competition, independent media and space to exercise civil liberties, among others (Akokpari 2010). I will, however, refrain from using standards of the US-based organisation that is Freedom House and instead choose other key features that may or may not include those of Freedom House but are essentially visible in an African setting. One has to establish a workable limit that I hope will still account for the key features of the FS methodology and enable the reader to locate him/herself as a leader of whatever institution across villages, provinces and nations. Equally, there are several conceptualisations of the selected terms of reference. I will not engage in lengthy discussions about which definition is better than another. The aim is for the reader to know exactly what I mean when I use this or that terminology.

A tradition as a term is used here interchangeably with culture. Understood as specific 'patterns of basic assumptions that a given group has invented, discovered, or developed… (Schein 1984, 6), this concept has been extensively theorised. There are national cultures (Hofstede 1991); power, achievement, role and support oriented cultures (Harrison 1979); club, task, role and existential cultures (Handy 1978); fragmented, mercenary, communal and networked cultures (Goffee and Jones 1998); and integration, differentiated and fragmented cultures (Martin 2002). Of particular interest here is Weiburst's (1989) conceptual analysis that led the author to distinguish three strands of traditions: historical, interpreted and contemporary. Historical tradition is, in this case, when one seeks to understand the world and the exact way in which African ancestors did and understood things. Interpreted tradition refers to tradition in as far as it is believed by a certain group to have taken place; and contemporary tradition is how tradition manifests itself in the way that people in contemporary times are living out their lives.

Education is an ambiguous term and people use it to mean different things. It can mean general lessons of life, or some degree of learning by animals (Carr 2003). I draw from Brock and Alexiadou (2013:1) for whom education comprises 'two basic activities: learning and teaching', to define it here as any form of socialisation (in whatever field) that can result in either deliberate or forced acquisition of knowledge.

Knowledge, therefore, is viewed here as the content of socialisation and, unlike Pring (1994; 1995), who thinks such content must be truth-focused instead of instrumental and must be obtained through broad initiation, here I take it to mean any understanding whether truth-focused or instrumental.

Legitimacy is another fluid term. With regard to the opinions of the masses, some think that 'the beliefs at any given time are not essential information for determining the system's legitimacy' (Rogowski 1974, Stephan 1992). Whether this view is held by those who fear that an overreliance on public opinion could lead to a grass root revolution is another matter. What is also true is that the public's disengagement with the running of their affairs could be comparable to a ship that is floating aimlessly because it has lost the necessary people who give the boat not only sailing weight but also direction. I use the term legitimacy to mean the genuine, popular sailing and directional weight an institution (people and policies) needs.

Legality on the other hand is the accountability that ensures all the processes as stipulated by the law(s), in a given entity, have been followed. Legality, however, does not automatically imply morality of a particular law or legal process.

Fear has been theorised extensively by Bauman (2006), for example. In his more than social enterprise, Bauman discusses fear holistically from, say, scholasticism to what he calls 'liquid' modern time. The project of conquering fear through science, it is remarked, yielded to nothing as 'our uncertainty: ...our ignorance of threats and of what is to be done – what can and

130

can't be – to stop it in its tracks – or to fight it back if stopping it is beyond our power' (ibid. 2) still persists.

Bauman goes on to agree with those who see 'fear' everywhere, before bringing another concept 'derivative fear', which, according to the author, is recycled fear that guides social and cultural actions. This is the view from a chaotically unstructured and irregular world of non-calculable dangers from sources that cannot be pinned down. But if we looked at Bauman's 'negatively globalised world' (ibid. 99) strictly from a social vantage point where there is structuration, with dangers/threats of course, 'fear' is first and foremost a feeling felt by subjects/individuals. It can be shared by a group of people, though not experienced in an identical way, as in fear of recession and terrorist attacks (from other individuals, structures and natural disasters, otherwise known as acts of God). But fear can also be projected to other bodies and spaces (be it humans, who might, for example, murder us; trees and meteorites that may crush us; and even the air, the next breath of which we breathe might just be the last, hence our preoccupation with air quality control etc.). When fear is either projected or already inhabiting those bodies and spaces, it does not remain as fear but becomes a threat, which ignites the feeling of fear towards them. Here, fear is not aimed at nothing; it has structure and/or agents as its referents. And it has reason to, given structure and agency's broken trust (see Chapter 2). The only trouble is that the feeler of fear is unsure about the force of threat, the time it will strike and also in what order.

Bauman also seems to discuss fear from an intrinsically conflictual world, where the chain reaction to feelings of fear is either flight or fight (if not overcome but perhaps stop it). Yet in an ontological world where subjects and structures need not be in a constant fight or flight mode but rather work collaboratively, then fear needs to be reconceptualised. Fear here is thought of as the certainty of the constraining hold/threats that structures can put on subjects to diminish their agentic force. Such a feeling can also be put on a sliding scale where we

131

can be certain if the fear level is low or high. Low fear exerted on agents (as medium) should automatically lead to high self-scrutinising structures as the outcome but that is not always the case, as I demonstrate when discussing quadrant 1. In the same way, high fear should lead to low self-scrutinising structures/institutions but that too is not always the case, as it shall be shown when discussing quadrant 3.

Self-Scrutiny, therefore, is the state of transparency and accountability that can be self-imposed and/or demanded by others, especially agents/subjects of institutions. The changing characteristics of institutional self-scrutiny in the face of dynamic agents will become clearer as I outline the methodology.

And finally, what do I mean by *FS (fear and self-scrutiny) methodology of structuration*? In previous chapters, I spoke of the duo 'fear and self-scrutiny' as my experience-based indicators of duality of structures. Such a representation can seem arbitrary. I therefore want to reiterate here that the FS methodology of structuration is rooted in the ontological status of the recursiveness between structure and agency. Freire (1996:107) echoed this when he called for transforming (recursive) actions, which 'cannot fail to assign the people a fundamental role in the transformation process'. The phrase 'transformation process' has the features of both movement and end or medium and outcome embedded in it. Such calls for twin reactions of medium and outcome have been exemplified in the actions of leaders, such as Nelson Mandela with the establishment of the truth and reconciliation commission (self-scrutiny) and the council of the 'elders' (fear), as already discussed.

Another point to bear in mind is that there have been other attempts to outline a methodology in the light of Giddens' structuration theory. Barley and Tolbert (1997), for example, have come up with a rich four-step procedure, which involves defining an institution at risk, charting a flow of actions, examining scripts for patterns of behaviour and linking findings.

132

I recommend that this and other step-by-step practical approaches be used not only to know reality for its own sake but also know it for a purpose. The FS methodology of structuration (of ntu), therefore, provides a way of knowing the features of interactions between institutions and subjects for the purpose of achieving real *ntu* ontology (structuration theory), which is value laden reality. While the evidence used to make the case for the FS methodology of structuration is mainly from Africa, I want the reader to appreciate its wider sociological implication in the debate about structure and agency. The FS methodology of structuration may not amount to the death of the dualism between structure and agency but I hope the reader will get a sense, as I did, of it becoming obsolete. In its unpopulated format, the FS methodology of structuration would appear as follows:

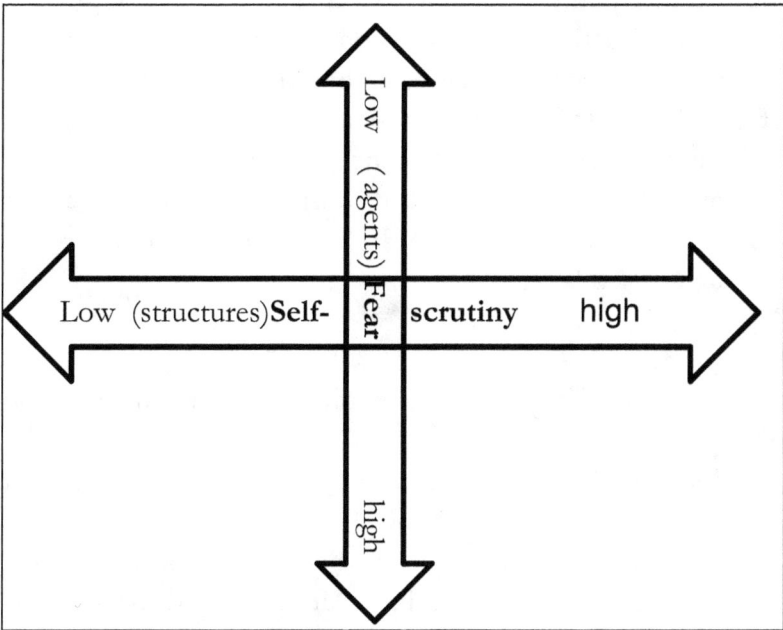

In the first edition, a lot of effort was expended on quadrant 4 and I will come back to it later. I will, however, start the discussion from quadrant 1 and onwards without necessarily suggesting that such is the natural movement or evolution within the overall model. In this explorative discussion, I will attempt to demonstrate what a low fear and low self-scrutiny environment, for example, looks like, especially in relation to the terms of reference and hopefully provide a comprehensive tool that can enable people to have a greater understanding of the (African) world and act accordingly, in order to effect change for the better. Ubuntu values of collectivism and humanism etc. (Littrell et al. 2013) and various contributions by Africans thus far are not neglected, as suggested by Kasanda's (2016) critique of this book. In response to such concerns, the FS model provides the basis on which to conceptualise those values as well as appreciate the empowering and constraining nature of various contributions whether it be by Africans or non-Africans (through aid, for example).

Quadrant 1 (Q1)

Let us describe a case that many, in Africa and the world over, would be familiar with.

Case study 1: 'My church pastor is a man of God, a great leader that I would trust with my life and all my possessions. He prays for me and instructs me on what to do according to what God through the bible tells him. Me on my part, I give my offerings, I don't ask what the pastor does with it, which would be like asking God to account for my gratitude when he gives me hundredfold'. It turns out that the pastor was in fact using a false sense of security to prey on poor believers to fund his expensive lifestyle. The uncertainty that continues to characterise post-colonial Africa has, in the case of Nigeria, resulted in fearful agents. Churches, therefore, provided that sanctuary of fearless security. While some are genuine, Marshall (1991) speaks of greedy pastors who would take advantage of this naïve trust of agents.

135

The above pattern of relationship can be applied to any field and there are several examples of theocratic African leaders who would borrow the church pastor's divine image. One of the slogans during Mobutu's time would literally be translated as 'power comes from God'. In any case, the important transferable elements are that the subjects have *low fear* in an institution that is *low on self-scrutiny*.

Now, how do the terms of reference discussed earlier apply to this low fear, low self-scrutiny setting? Education, I would argue, is nothing other than indoctrination where learning as a process and outcome are substituted for instant revealed knowledge that comes in the form of commandments. The idea of revelatory epistemology, that Luyaluka (2016) argues to be the basis of African indigenous knowledge, has to be understood using the fear and self-scrutiny methodology of Ubuntu within which such 'revealed knowledge' is received and operationalised in the (African) social world. Unlike in quadrant 4, where (African) social life is at its best, here leaders use such academic theorising to advance a style of leadership that is covertly dehumanising. Subjects are not allowed to question how the commandments came about, as the process of revelation is a 'divine' mystery that is backed by some authoritative sources (text or person), often failing to stand the scrutiny of the context of the referenced texts, as echoed in the report *Inside the Jihadi Mind* (2015). The outcome may not be what you want but you do not complain. Instead, you remain grateful for God's (the leader's) providence. The commandments effectively become the divine laws that should make subjects' actions legal and legitimate when interacting with their structures and carrying out commands. Those actions are usually demands for (more) prayers for the leaders' good health and wisdom so that he or she can steer the institution in the 'right' direction, which, in most cases, turns out to be the leaders' unscrutinised ideology, interpretations and opulent lifestyles. The guiding question is always 'What is God telling you?' and the image I give to this quadrant is 'baby-snake rapport'. Baby is chosen in the sense that this human entity is usually fearless in front of the poisonous creature that in reality is ruthless but outwardly harmless to children, as long as no-one seeks to scrutinise it.

In keeping with the spirit of this quadrant, the reader must allow me to issue a fatwa: this quadrant should not be taken to represent African traditional kingdoms etc. in a wholesale manner. A dictum in Socrates' Apology has it that 'the unexamined life is not worth living for a human being'. The categorisations within this methodological model, therefore, are aimed at enabling an African to examine his/her past, present and future, in order not only to situate the social formation of reality but also to engage with its (de)formation and reformation.

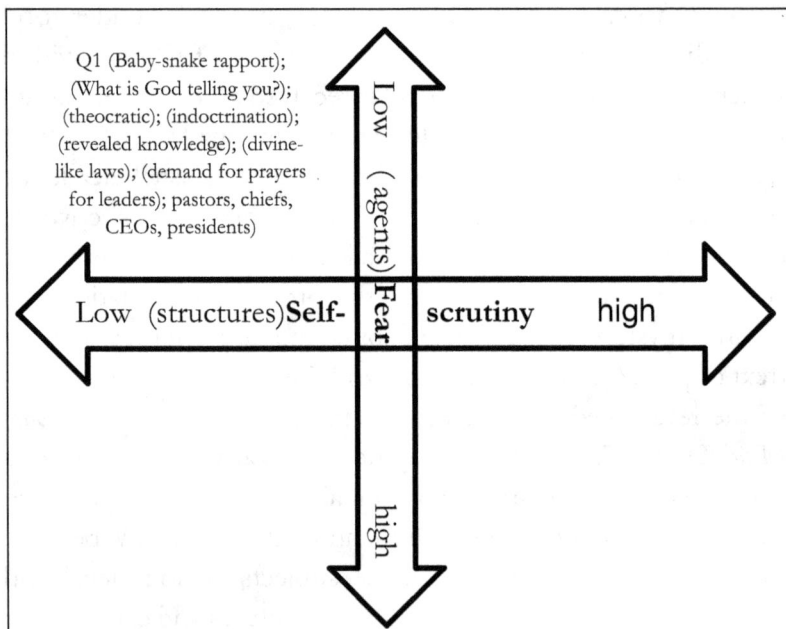

Q1 (Baby-snake rapport); (What is God telling you?); (theocratic); (indoctrination); (revealed knowledge); (divine-like laws); (demand for prayers for leaders); pastors, chiefs, CEOs, presidents)

Low (agents) Fear

high

Low (structures)Self-   scrutiny   high

Quadrant 2 (Q2)

I will anonymise personal information about this particular case study to protect anyone from harm. That said; the culture is so widespread that it may not matter describing what is common knowledge, as long as individual names are withheld.

Case study 2: 'Person A tells a stranger, person B: look, I had to sell my concept for a community regeneration project to the government authorities first before a foreign body would fund it. The authorities liked it and officially sent me an invitation to discuss the project further. After the positive initial meeting, I never heard from them again until I realised that the same project had been highjacked and branded as a new innovation by the country's president. (…) Person B responds by asking: what are you going to do about it? Person A says: I could contact my lawyer, or speak out through the media but I won't even dare do that, I don't want to die that early'.

Once again, this story is not exclusive to Africa and people having to bite their tongues about disputed authorship of certain materials, for fear of perhaps losing their jobs, can apply to schools, hospitals, churches, and journalism. Here, power that should warrant this level of *low self-scrutiny* does not necessarily come from God, since the leader himself/herself is portrayed as God. During Mobutu's brutal rule of the then Zaire, he was shown on national television to be descending from the clouds (for many thought to be the home of God, making him effectively God). 'After God came the king. Today we have no kings; it is the president [leader] who replaced them…' laments one African resident (Guardian 2016). The personality cult around leaders, who desperately seek to mystify their offices through the use of superlatives like 'supreme leader' and come across as enigmatic, become the rule of thumb even for those leaders, like Muammar Gaddafi, who claimed to be religious. Here, name change may not acquire the same holiness that a bishop gets when he abandons his old name and chooses a new one upon assuming the papacy, but an additional name for such leaders serves a similar purpose. Whether the leader does change his/her name (as is the case with some leaders) or not, agents with an obscured or absently present low fear would compound institutional low self-scrutiny by changing their names to win favours, hence: 'I had to change my name to sound like that of the university president to stand a chance of admission' or 'I had to use my wife's name who is from the president's tribe in order to have our application to have electricity wired to our home granted quickly' some of my informants confessed.

It would be inaccurate to limit this scenario of name changing due to 'high fear and low self-scrutiny' only to Africa. It has, under a different guise, happened in 21st century Europe, as the following case shows and could happen anywhere else: 'a black African David's marriage with a white Dutch ex-wife Di hits the rocks and it ends acrimoniously. Both David and Di went on to develop new friendships which ended in marriage with their new partners. Since breaking up with David, Di has always had custody of their two children with David. After applying to a Dutch court, Di got permission to replace the children's African surname they got through David with Di's new Dutch husband's name. The judge, it would appear, found it valid Di's (high) fear that the children would be discriminated against later in life if they carried their African names when applying for jobs etc.'

To return to the African context, divine revelations are replaced by human orders, which, in the wake of independence (and in some/most cases up until now), were presented as a return to authenticity and a truly African way of life. Such an aspiration was noble, through not clearly elaborated as *ntu* in the way that is approached here in Q4. With a twisted understanding of authenticity or historical tradition, people were/are instead being indoctrinated, as the following extract will show. "It's like (name of an African president) has indoctrinated people because: there is no running water, no electricity, no roads and no one knows how the country is run but people still go and 'vote' for him". Indoctrination is a predominant characteristic of Q1 and 2; even though that does not necessarily mean it does not occur elsewhere, as the following paragraph shows.

Let us start from the premise that no institution or (African) country would like to be described in Q1, 2 and 3 terms, which may not necessarily be consistent with the actual reality on the

139

ground. Given South Africa's association with ntu prototype leader Mandela, for example, the country could claim the moral high ground of being the bedrock of Q4 (ntu) leadership. However, still within that geographical space, there has been a king who, while loved by low fear agents, used his unscrutinised institutional powers in 2015 to ignite xenophobic feelings among black South Africans, which then resulted in despicable attacks on foreign black residents in South Africa, who subsequently began to live in high fear. If we look across the Atlantic and hypothetically argue that the USA had borrowed African key building blocks of ntu leadership to be where it is today (the land of the free and home of the brave, according to Pope Francis's 2015 opening speech to congress), there are nevertheless signs of home grown pockets of non-ntu leadership and citizenship, which manifest themselves through indoctrination and then (racial, political, religious…) radicalisation/terrorism (Vertigans 2007).

Education in Q2 is not based on the process of working out the solutions to the problems facing structures and agency since the outcomes or solutions (highjacked or not) come in the form of orders that have to be executed without questioning how we got there. Just like person B in the above case study, agents are charged with *high fear* for their lives. They may not know the extent and timing of the threat but they know that structure is its potential ruthless source. You may not have broken any particular known rule but here legality and legitimacy are the leader's imposed doctrines. If challenged, which is (un)likely, the key question/response would be 'did you do what I told you?' The image for this quadrant is 'lion-goat rapport'.

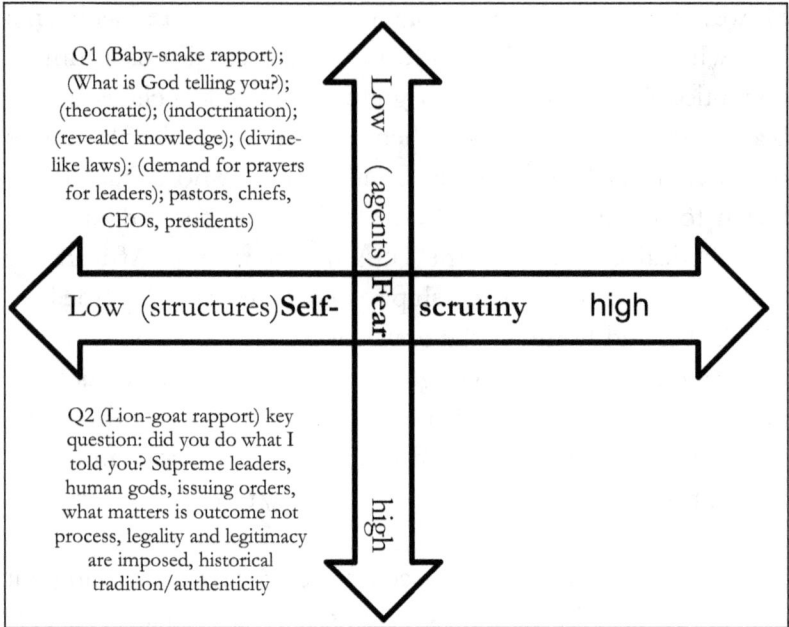

Q1 (Baby-snake rapport);
(What is God telling you?);
(theocratic); (indoctrination);
(revealed knowledge); (divine-
like laws); (demand for prayers
for leaders); pastors, chiefs,
CEOs, presidents

Low (agents) Fear

Low (structures)**Self-** scrutiny high

Q2 (Lion-goat rapport) key
question: did you do what I
told you? Supreme leaders,
human gods, issuing orders,
what matters is outcome not
process, legality and legitimacy
are imposed, historical
tradition/authenticity

Quadrant 3 (Q3)

Case study 3: Here, the reader is invited to reconsider case study 2, especially the part in parentheses (...), where I deliberately withheld some information to make the case for this **high fear** but a **biased** kind of **high self-scrutiny**. 'Person B asked: is that all they had to say without any proof? Person A: I went back to ask them what happened but I was told that someone else had apparently submitted a similar idea just a few days earlier than me but it allegedly had been lost in the system momentarily. They showed me some letters which they claim proves their position but I know it's transparency with a small (t)'.

Despite being convinced about the opacity of the institutional process defended by the so called 'experts', who presumably can prove anything, the agent like in Q2, is still living in high fear of intimidation, arbitrary arrests/imprisonment and even death/assassinations. In this quadrant, the leader avoids being seen to give orders. He or she would go to great lengths either to explain or delegate that responsibility to a spokesperson or biased media to explain the process whose outcome was already determined. It is a bit like arriving at an interview where you are told everything about the organisation, and put through a supposedly rigorous process but the job is already someone else's from the word go. Those with an obscured sense of agency do not act but instead coat the lack of transparency with their high fear. Brave agents (or disadvantaged interview candidates in the case shown below) could dare to question the process, in an effort to drag the agent to low fear and the institution to high self-scrutiny. To illustrate this point, I present a letter written by 'I' to 'A'. 'I' and 'C' had turned up for an interview at location 'D' where 'B' worked under 'A'.

Date

Dear Mr A,

Thank you for yesterday's feedback and as you may have sensed I was disappointed not to have been offered the opportunity.

I have had to carefully word this letter so that I don't sound bitter, which I am not; and that I do not burn a possible bridge and that's how much I admire your leadership and how you and your team have brought staff and students to commit to a set of learning principles. That's why even if a job went up tomorrow in your institution, I would still apply.

However, I needed to formally relay my concern. B knew C as a friend and they pray at the same Church. B invited C to spend a day at D (B's workplace) and C was rumoured to be the preferred candidate prior to the selection process. It would only have been fair for everybody's sake for B to be asked to step aside.

I take your point that you made sure that you grilled C too. I believe you and that's how much I have confidence in you. But that's my subjective opinion. To anyone who does not know you or, let us say, if you were put in my position, I am convinced you would still have the objective question mark whether the process was at all a fair one.

I threw everything at it to get that post that even if I were going against a minister for education or a consultant like C, I was still hopeful to get it especially knowing that the job was advertised as a teacher of xxx. Although C's consultancy experience tipped it his way, but there were a lot of other things that could have tipped it my way too: for example the fact that I have x and x degrees and C does not. I know you have the right to apply your own criteria in the end, and rather than make it about my other colleague, whom I wish well, I just wanted to honestly share with you, as I would do with anyone, my concern.

I have copied E because you had to consult her to arrive at your decision and I have copied B too.

I appreciated you wishing me, AND MY FAMILY, well. Thank you for that and I would like to do the same for all three of you.

Sincerely yours,

'T'.

With the above experience in mind, it feels convenient here to state the image I have reserved for this quadrant, which is 'snail-dog race rapport'. The two are conveniently and 'fairly' given the opportunity to compete and go through a process whose outcome is a forgone conclusion.

I have, in previous chapters, challenged Giddens' suggestion that democracy started in the west. But many would agree that there was a time, in the 1990s, when modern democracy as a western movement swept across the African continent disrupting certain practices. That disruption can be characterised on two levels: materially and symbolically. Material disruption was witnessed in the destruction in terms of human lives lost and protests that led to widespread looting and burning of people's (ill-gotten or ethically acquired) goods. Conflicts of interest meant that national dialogues had to be called, which, in my analysis, leads to the second disruption. Symbolic disruption is the view that the demands from agents to have a say in the running of their countries may have yielded something, but only symbolically, as the legitimate rhetoric among Africans and Africanists about the need for Africans' own brand of democracy grew stronger. Such a development brought to prominence a breed of legalists and constitutionalists who were/are indeed extreme relativists.

Those constitutionalists are the ones who contribute to national dialogues, where they would (intentionally or not but conveniently nonetheless) leave ambiguous statements that they would seek to reinterpret in favour of a particular person/leader or leadership practices. Let us take the case of the 2015 presidential elections crisis in Burundi, where the president had served 'two terms' but technically only one where he was elected DIRECTLY by the people according to article 7 of the constitutional principles of the post-transition constitution of the Arusha peace and reconciliation agreement for Burundi. Legally, he was still due a second term of direct universal suffrage. Already in this quadrant, legality is the preferred mantra at the expense of legitimacy. Fed up with endless military coups, African regional bodies such as the African Union (AU) have also fallen into the same trap of defending the indefensible, where they ask for a return to the rule of what is essentially 'compromised' law.

Even though high fear is still the ultimate weapon, unless the primary change agents (the people) make the leader succumb to pressure, such as in the case of former president Blaise Compaoré, who unsuccessfully sought a third term by wanting to change the constitution legally, the other weapon is that leaders in this quadrant bank on a tiresome drawn out process causing presumably 'fearful' agents to give in and accept some form of compromise that still gives them some role within the shaping and reshaping of institutions. What matters for leaders in this quadrant is the process as the outcome is already determined. Imagine being given a simple mathematical equation of 4 + 4 and the teacher gives you a formula but he or she knows that the answer in the end is 18. You, as the reader, must be wondering why 18 instead of 8. Now, this is how it works when process takes priority over outcome. Where the constitution allows a candidate only two 4 year terms, they will take that, knowing full well that it will be 18 in total, since at the end of the second term another process will change the constitution to allowing a 5 year term, which the incumbent wins twice (fairly or unfairly) to make it 18 years and, as agents begin to care less, the cap is lifted to allow 'innate' leaders to rule for life.

'Managers *do things right/correctly* while leaders *do the right thing*' (Slaughter 2012:85). That means, when the law does not allow anyone to hold unlicensed protest, a peacefully protesting group of unpaid teachers, who congregate in front of a ministry, do not have to be flushed out by teargas for breaking the law and asked to protest correctly by applying for permission to protest, which they will not be given for some biased reason. A leader would do the right thing in this case. This quadrant is mainly led by managers who are eager to stick to the law when its interpretation suits them. They are legalists but show openness to change, so that, for example, when president Uhuru (without necessarily pigeonholing his leadership to this quadrant) was asked about his administration's position on gay rights during a press conference with the US President Barack

145

Obama, he did not refer to Kenyan law and culture but responded diplomatically in a way that showed openness to the interpretation of the law with 'it's a non-issue in Kenya right now and it's a question of priorities'. Suggesting that maybe in future it could be open to discussion. This was quite a significant shift that was missed by the media, who focused instead on Africa versus the West with 'Uhuru clashes with Obama on gay rights' as a headline. Such an attitude, together with a country like South Africa which has gone as far as legalising gay marriage, approaches tradition not historically but as interpreted and, perhaps, as it manifests itself in contemporary times.

Ultimately, because Q3 leaders are legalists, resigning from a position is a non-issue as long as they have not broken any rule or law as they interpret them. Hence, the charges of bringing a profession into disrepute or undermining the integrity of an office do not stick if they can technically make you believe that they are doing things right.

Caution is needed not to treat all lawyers and constitutionalists as in league with the leaders in quadrant 3, as all quadrants have their own kinds of legalists driven by a different kind of FS methodology of structuration (the *ntu* methodology). Therefore, in the interest of the continuity of the discourse, *Constitutional Democracy in Africa* (Nwabueze 1984) should not be seen as running against the FS methodology of structuration. In my view, the sort of legalists described by the author can fit well within quadrant 4, which will be discussed next.

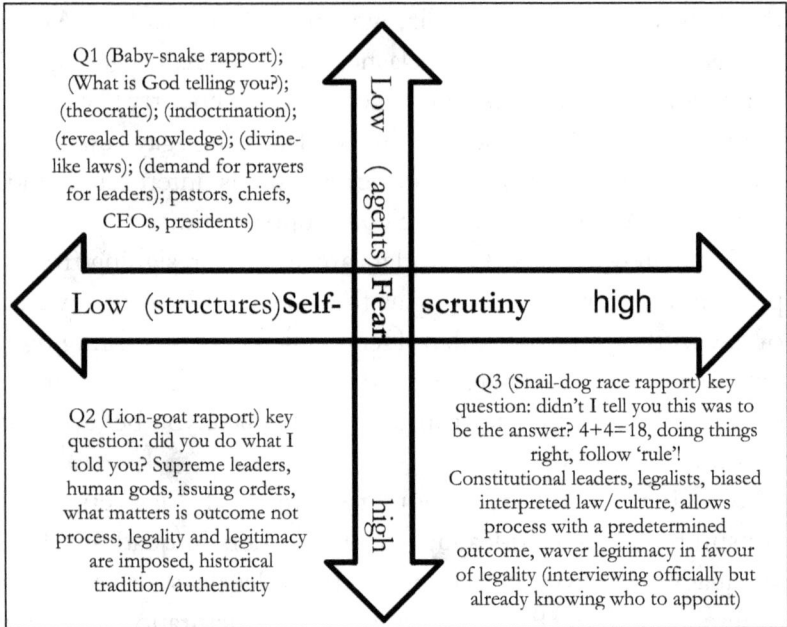

Q1 (Baby-snake rapport); (What is God telling you?); (theocratic); (indoctrination); (revealed knowledge); (divine-like laws); (demand for prayers for leaders); pastors, chiefs, CEOs, presidents)

Low (agents) Fear high

Low (structures)Self- scrutiny high

Q2 (Lion-goat rapport) key question: did you do what I told you? Supreme leaders, human gods, issuing orders, what matters is outcome not process, legality and legitimacy are imposed, historical tradition/authenticity

Q3 (Snail-dog race rapport) key question: didn't I tell you this was to be the answer? 4+4=18, doing things right, follow 'rule'! Constitutional leaders, legalists, biased interpreted law/culture, allows process with a predetermined outcome, waver legitimacy in favour of legality (interviewing officially but already knowing who to appoint)

I will make two overall remarks about Q1, 2 and 3. 1) Even though poverty can be found in a typical *ntu* leadership quadrant (Q4 below), it is most endemic in Q1, 2 and 3 dominated environments. Some have sought to explain poverty from a purely psychological perspective (Puplampu 2013). While such theorising enriches our understanding, it is legitimate to think that psychological transactions stem from and impact on an ontological reality of a given modality or interaction point between an institution and its subjects. 2) Even though agents are not given a fair chance to shape their institutions, such an opportunity is not completely removed from them. In the chaos, deception and struggle, agents too, just like institutions, have acted inappropriately (have betrayed trust) as already discussed in Chapter 2. An additional remark concerns Q3 in particular. There is a sense that leaders in Q3 exercise a soft form of deception, where they use physical force only to defend their biased 'high-scrutiny' arguments. This should be read in conjunction with the assertion that 'there is no crueller tyranny than that which is perpetuated under the shield of the law and in the name of justice' (Montesquieu 1721).

Quadrant 4 (Q4)

I will summarise a published piece of literature as a case study for this quadrant seen here as the defining features of African philosophy and sociology on which to base a people's citizenship and leadership ideals/practices. The literature uses a leadership practice called *Barza* in the Eastern Democratic Republic of Congo (DRC) as a successful and then failed conflict resolution mechanism. The main reason for using this example is to highlight how *Barza* is founded on *ntu* ontology when it worked and like quadrant 1, 2 or 3 when it failed. It also reiterates the continuity between traditional and modern African practices.

The DRC colonial rule was uniquely brutal. That was followed by 32 years of dictatorship by Mobutu, who was deposed by Laurent Désiré Kabila (LDK) with the backing of Congo's Eastern neighbouring countries (Rwanda and Uganda), which (genuinely or not) were ridding the Eastern Congo of its remnant Hutu militias responsible for the 1994 Rwandan genocide. LDK then fell out with his sponsors resulting in further armed conflicts that drew in many African countries and ultimately led to LDK's assassination. Joseph Kabila took over the reins of power and has since been through some disputed electoral cycles. It is in that context that Clark (2008) uses his article to assess the impact of *Barza* as an institution for community conflict resolution in the Eastern part of the DRC. *Barza* originates from Swahili *Baraza* which means 'Verandah', as a meeting place for the village elders to solve problems and there have been similar practices in Rwanda with *Gacaca*, and in Northern Uganda with *mato oput* and *gamo tong*. In Eastern Congo,

> the *Barza* assembles leaders from North Kivu's (*one of the provinces at the time of Clark's writing of his article –my italics*) nine major ethnic groups: Hunde, Hutu, Kano, Kumu, Nande, Nyanga, Tembo, Tutsi and Twa to discuss issues central to community life and to help resolve low-level conflicts before they escalate to violence (ibid 1).

Clark does not link the *Barza* with the Ubuntu leadership often associated with Africa but equates it to Gacaca that Bangura (2008a) sees as related to Ubuntu. Besides, the two fundamental features of *ntu* methodology of structuration (self-scrutiny and fear) can be identified in Clarks' (ibid 7) description of the *Barza*:

Within the Barza itself, its leaders claim to foster an environment of open dialogue to serve as a model of ethnic cooperation throughout North Kivu. '[W]e preach . . . sincerity and frankness, we don't hide anything,' said Thomas Kibira Katarungu, from the Nyanga community and former president of the Barza. 'This inspires us and teaches members of other ethnic groups who live with us here in the town a lesson.

Transparency, or *high self-scrutiny,* teaches a lesson, which I would say is more engaged, peaceful and whose agents have *low fear.* I will return to this case study later, if only to make the point about how the *Barza* leaned towards Q1, 2 and 3 and effectively veered off the fourth quadrant's defining features of high self-scrutiny and low fear.

What one might notice, in terms of how some of the terms of reference apply here, is that leaders who are in tune with this quadrant will not depend on revealed or imposed knowledge, but rather act according to a process that will deliver the desired outcomes. To put it another way, they will agree on the outcomes and collaboratively work together to achieve them. The use of trans-situational primary knowledge and secondary knowledge (expertise) on the basis of one's subjectivity, innovation, developmental learning and emergence of local theories, as discussed in Chapter 4, are brought into play in a Barza/Ubuntu/structuration theory atmosphere of low fear and high self-scrutiny. Leaders here do not only rely on legality but also legitimacy, which is granted by the sailing and directional weight/support of the agents. They want to not only do things correctly but also do the right thing. I will use some contemporary African examples to illustrate a few statements that have just been made.

There might be widespread consensus about one of the personalities to be mentioned shortly, but for the rest the reader needs to remember that examples to illustrate some of the key features of any quadrant can be slippery and I have no vested interest in elevating this or that person, other than to use particular examples of their leadership displaying certain desirable features I believe we want to see more of in Africa (*ntu* leadership).

Since independence decrees were signed in the 1960s, questions have been raised as to whether some countries, such as the DRC, were prepared enough to assume various responsibilities (Clark 2002). Hence, some things may be legal but a question about whether it is the right thing at this time is another matter. In its recent history, in 2015, the DRC was also faced with such questions when the existing 11 provinces were fragmented into 26. The country was struggling to organise a series of elections and some wondered whether the added costs of creating additional provinces was the right thing to do. The other camp, however, insisted on the fact that it was enshrined in the 2006 constitution, and therefore a legally binding prerogative that had to be implemented. Leaders in Q4 will ensure that what they are doing is not only legal but also right at a given time.

In previous chapters, I have used the case of Nelson Mandela's organisation of the truth and reconciliation commission and the group called 'the elders' to illustrate high self-scrutiny and low fear. Here, I will use his example of running for one term when he could have won a second or even third term if he wanted to be a Q1, 2, &3 kind of leader. Mandela would have stopped being an *ntu* leader, in the same way that the *Barza*, according to Clark (2008, 8), failed when, among other things, 'the Barza was simply a means for the rebels to ensconce sympathetic leadership at the grassroots level'. This is not to say that only structures are capable of derailing the *ntu* agenda in Q4. In the '*Unexpected Homecoming*' (Elonga Mboyo 2015), I narrate a story of a presumably Q4 head teacher's (representing the institution) failed bid to appoint a black teacher to counter his suspicion of systemic racism that had come to be defended by the employees (subjects) on the selection panel.

If followed through, the Senegalese president Macky Sall's announcement that he wanted to reduce presidential terms of office from 7 to 4 years, when he was only in his first term, is an example of just such a leadership that focuses on doing the right thing in the interest of the masses and thus wins a leader both legality and legitimacy.

Here, leaders demystify leadership, as they are able to assume their humanity like everybody else while transparently tackling the complex issues of leadership. 'One thing I like with Uhuru is that he has demystified the presidency' a Kenyan spoke

151

of his president. The guiding question for the leaders in this quadrant is 'what can we do? When matched with consistent actions, the institutions will be a reflection of the wishes of the people. It is not excluded that tolerance of freedom, consideration, integration and persuasiveness (Littrell et al. 2013) become part of leadership behaviours. Bound by Ubuntu's tenets of interdependence, as outlined here, longstanding (African) societal behaviours (values) of hospitality, generosity, collectivism and humanism (Littrell et al. 2013) find their fulfilment in this quadrant and effectively overcome the criticism of being a romantic communal thought that conceals power/resource inequalities (Kirk and Bolden 2006). The image that I believe encapsulates Q4 is that of a 'chameleon', to represent institutions that reflect the colour (actions) of its surrounding (agents/citizens) as shown in the figure below. And to reinforce Freire's (1970) point yet again, the Chameleon is the body or institution that 'cannot fail to assign the people a fundamental role in the transformation process', that of determining the colours of the Chameleon. That is the effect that high self-scrutinising institutions (secular or not) have on low fear agents and vice versa.

Q1 (Baby-snake rapport); (What is God telling you?); (theocratic); (indoctrination); (revealed knowledge); (divine-like laws); (demand for prayers for leaders); pastors, chiefs, CEOs, presidents)	Low (agents) Fear	Q4 (chameleon-environment rapport) Key question: what can we do? Doing the right thing! Genuine dialogue; process and outcome hence ensuring legitimacy and legality. 4+4=8. Agents shape traditions in their historical, interpreted and contemporary forms
Low (structures)Self-	scrutiny high	
Q2 (Lion-goat rapport) key question: did you do what I told you? Supreme leaders, human gods, issuing orders, what matters is outcome not process, legality and legitimacy are imposed, historical tradition/authenticity	high	Q3 (Snail-dog race rapport) key question: didn't I tell you this was to be the answer? 4+4=18, doing things right, follow 'rule'! Constitutional leaders, legalists, biased interpreted law/culture, allows process with a predetermined outcome, waver legitimacy in favour of legality (interviewing officially but already knowing who to appoint)

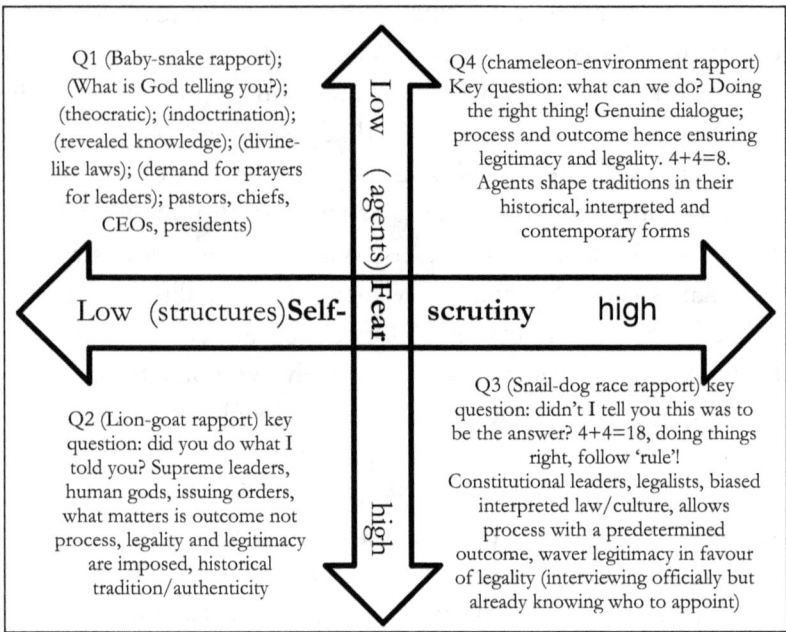

When Asante (1987:6) defines Afrocentricity as 'placing African ideals at the centre of any analysis that involves African culture and behaviour'; such a call is being heeded here through the FS model, which provides the framework where those ideals can emerge (Q4) or not (Q 1, 2 and 3). Personal reservations about witchcraft and sorcery…aside, such beliefs and others, I would argue, find their constraining and empowering capacity or, in Tempels' (1959) usage, diminish or strengthen 'life force' within this overall sociological interplay between structure and agency. I also want to argue tentatively that Molefi Asante's (1987) characterisation of Afrocentricity as human conditions of feeling, knowing and acting, Mazama's (2001) categories of the cognitive, structural and functional aspects of Afrocentricity, and Dei's (1994) analysis that led to the identification of solidarity, mutuality, collective responsibility, gerontocracy, gender equality and many others are the historical by-products of the ongoing Afrocentric ontological narrative as defined in the FS model, which may have started off from a Eurocentric

153

thought called structuration theory but, as defended here, is commensurate with Ubuntu. It is this ongoing interdependent dialogue between force-beings that overcomes the criticism of Ubuntu as humanism that seems 'unable to be open to the possibility that newcomers might radically alter our understanding of what it means to be human' (Higgs 2012:49).

However, what academics and leaders can do is facilitate the pressing of certain historical by-products of Afrocentricity into perpetuity within an Ubuntu environment of low fear and high self-scrutiny, as well as engage in further empirical studies to describe and explain future manifestations of the methodology of structuration (of Ubuntu). It is also becoming more pertinent to engage in a worldwide study of what is actually being taught in universities with a focus on African studies, so that we can gain a clearer idea about the historical by-products of Afrocentricity that are being stressed. Keskin (2014) has already made a useful contribution in that sense. However, more work is needed in the light of the FS methodology of Ubuntu (structuration).

This analysis also has wider implications with the whole sociological enterprise that seeks not only to characterise what reality is but also attempts to study concepts such as culture. In the light of the methodology of Ubuntu, it has become pertinent to requalify ontologically/methodologically the sharp contrasts of individualistic versus communitarian, feminine versus masculine cultures... (Hofstede 1991). Let us say for example that 'community cultures' work with a certain degree of collegiality. The concept of contrived collegiality (Hargreaves 2003) that I referred to in the first chapter, is further evidence that, in the light of the methodology of Ubuntu, there is going to be an element of collegiality in all four quadrants and that researchers need to illuminate us on the ontological underpinnings of a specific field using this methodological approach.

Even if it is accepted that 'our human sense of self is irreducible to our sociality' (Archer 2002:13), such unmediated

154

existence of the 'I', in relation to structure, can be said to be in a state of silence akin to fearless agents who, in this case, completely depend on the trust narrative of structure (see Chapter 2) to deliver high rather than low scrutiny. In keeping with Archer's logic, since the 'I' is also a continuous reflexive self, it can break its silence and actively engage with structure when it assumes a social identity.

Tribe (alism) and Ethics

The FS model is not a Meta-methodology. That, however, does not imply that we should tame our sense of adventure in order to understand the world better. I have therefore chosen to understand tribalism, and some of the conflicts around it, as a testing example of the model. The term tribalism can be used to refer to the state or fact of being organised as a tribe or tribes (Banks 1996). That can imply identity and positivity. It can also, as witnessed in some places in Africa, be the source of discrimination and discord.

Using the adapted FS model to analyse a single issue of tribe below, I want to posit that tribalism manifests itself differently and we can use the FS methodology of structuration/Ubuntu to understand the different manifestations.

Q1 Tribe	Q4 Tribe
Q2 Tribe	Q3 Tribe

To be organised as a 'tribe' refers to an affinity that is not exclusive to the traditional usage of the concept in the African context. In the modern 'age of the tribe', such affinity can, thanks to new technologies, form anywhere on the basis of one's political/religious convictions, sex, music, sport... (Maffesoli 1996; Tyldesley 2013). However, in Q1, tribalism would be wrapped in low fear and low self-scrutiny. This is the scenario where a group of people, within the safety of their home, church, territory, would entertain expressed and unexpressed thoughts that would make them feel like they are the chosen people. They would also enjoy unscrutinised institutional backing from pastors, leaders etc. The clothing, songs, food and little habits of the group become the dogma, but only in their own confined safe spaces. Similarly, the 'unchosen tribe' can feel at ease with their structural status, again still within their secure quarters. Those familiar with the film 'Coach Carter' will grasp this better, where subjects of a 'unchosen race', would make jokes about their status by calling themselves 'niggers'. They muse about their 'unchosen' ethnicity on buses, trains, on the farm, while waiting for an additional dose of the same thing from like-minded people and structures. At this stage of self-aggrandisement and self-deprecation, tribalism is only a cosy alienating phenomenon. It only gets a little dangerous and a source of discord in Q2 and 3.

In Q2, a tribe is not only a chosen people; others begin or are made to feel inferior and disadvantaged too. That feeling can be imagined or real but the fear of the threat is high and often met with institutions that are defensive, unscrutinised and in denial. In Q3, the agents feel the same way as in Q2 but institutions here are beginning to self-scrutinise, only in as far as they can rationalise and justify the agents' high fear as either unfounded psychological/cultural bias on the part of the fearing agents or simply by pointing to some weaknesses of figures of the 'disadvantaged' tribe and the strengths of some members of the 'advantaged' tribe to justify certain tribal imbalance.

Kinship ties that are manipulated and result in ethnic violence and tyranny in Q2 and 3 have long dominated the discourse around the 'tribe', characterising it as a pre-human banality of the African, as opposed to the culture of civilisation of the West. That has prompted reactions describing the idea of tribe as a Eurocentric misrepresentation of the African reality (Ray 2008). The view taken from the methodology of Ubuntu as presented here is to say that the Eurocentric (mis)representation of the tribe needs to see beyond Q2 and 3, in order to grasp the richness of this concept in Q4. The tribe is not a fixed entity, in the same way that Christian (2013:15) describes the Bedouin tribe identity as 'psychological and emotional imprinting of existential logic, geology and morality that may or may not be subject to adaptation'. While aiming to rehabilitate the concept of the 'tribe', the Afrocentric person also needs to acknowledge its low points (in Q1, 2 and 3) within the overall methodology of Ubuntu. As already discussed in Chapter 2, with regard to the Rwandan genocide, greed and other political motives were also responsible for the violence. That, however, should not be used to ignore the methodological structuration of tribe that led to violence in Q2 and 3. When discussing the 2007 post-election violence in Kenya, Ibelema's (2014: 175) assertion that among other things, '...ethnic rivalry and resentment were obvious components of the bloodshed...' gives credence to the case being put forward here.

In Q4, tribalism is not shied away from. The tribe is an identity that is talked about and celebrated within the recognition of the wealth and diversity of a multi-coloured/cultured arena. Low fearing agents challenge what they see as Q1, 2 and 3 characteristics of tribalism. Self-scrutinising institutions do not only seek to defend themselves, they also ensure that processes reflect outcomes; and when they do not, various conciliatory and emancipatory measures are put in place to overcome certain imbalances. This is what would have led Berkeley (2001: 84) to argue that rather than being fixed to one's tribe, 'Africans in ever greater numbers favour ethnic and racial tolerance, the rule of law and sanctity of individual rights'. This is the sphere of the Barza, where inter-tribal/ethnic conflicts are resolved within the core Ubuntu tenets of low fear and high self-scrutiny.

A brief note on the moral basis or ethics that are pervasive within the FS model is necessary. I will use Ogundele and Hassan's (2013) discussion to point out that egoism is the moral determining factor throughout Q1, 2 and 3. This is when one's actions are undertaken only on the basis of one or a few others' interest. The utilitarian, justice and right theories of ethics, which seek fairness for all with a climate of low fear for agents and high self-scrutiny for institutions, are vastly reserved to Q4. Looking at Africa in general and Nigeria in particular, the above authors highlight corruption as one of the ethical problems facing Nigerian society and institutions. I would, however, encourage researchers to use the FS model to understand these ethical issues even further. I believe that corruption does manifest itself differently in Q1, 2, and 3. I will not engage in an endless analysis of various issues here but let me just point out one example. In *The Unexpected Homecoming* (Elonga Mboyo 2015), I document an incident where corruption is rationalised and interpreted, especially by those representing institutions, as **motivation**. Late President Mobutu (of Zaire - present DRC) once asked his fellow countrymen to steal but to do so sparingly or just a little, and it is often argued, in a self-defensive way, that the West should not give lessons on corruption, after all, there is corruption everywhere and the term has either English or French origins, which shows its Western origin. This perverted institutional interpretation of something bad to justify certain practices, amid high fears/worries of agents, is ontologically characteristic of Q3 features. Having outlined the FS model, and if you have followed my advice, now is the time to revisit Chapter 6 for a greater appreciation of how the African body can be (has been) treated under Q1, 2, 3 and 4.

What is movement like within the FS model?

Among the many good speeches he delivered, one famous global leader also said 'I wanted to come here because Africa is on the move' and went on to add 'people are being lifted out of poverty, income is up and the middle class is growing' (Barack Obama, 25/7/2015, speaking to business entrepreneurs during his historic visit to Kenya as the president of the United States).

Political rhetoric needs to stack up to the theoretical, sociological, cultural, ontological and, in this case, the *ntu* (FS methodology of Ubuntu) realities. Failure to do so imbues speeches designed to inspire the masses with a neo-liberal capitalist agenda, glossed over with soundbites and famous faces like the (then) president of the United States. Admittedly, I look up to him but this only obscures the journey and runs the risk of distracting people from the real trends of positive movement. As an example, the two biggest economies in Africa, South Africa and Nigeria, respectively recorded 53% and 13% 15-24 year old youth unemployment in 2013 (World Bank 2015)

Every quadrant, as discussed above, has a middle class of some sort and some people will be lifted out of poverty anyhow. However, behind such big headlines lie important questions, such as 'who are these people called middle class?' and 'who is the owner of this or that skyscraper, new supermall and so on and so forth?' In Q4, where there is high self-scrutiny, you are likely to get a straight answer. In Q1, 2 and 3 you are unlikely to get any clarity as not only is statistical data unavailable; everything is done in pitch-black divine secrecy and with biased justifications. The chances are that wealth is actually being concentrated by a select few whose empires are growing ever bigger, making it look like there is an irreversible boom for many. Vague soundbites like 'people are being lifted out of poverty' without concrete statistical figures (men versus women, young versus old, regions versus regions, …) and the great majority of people feeling it is not worth mentioning, even if it is intended to motivate people. Rather, it could have rather the adverse effect of appearing patronising and condescending. It needs to be said that this is not just about political leadership practices. Schools, for instance, have to adhere to the triangulation of data to show utmost transparency, in the way that students of different social categories are making progress, and at the same time have low fear when demanding their recompense.

Further research but most importantly low fear, is required to demand more self-scrutiny to ensure that institutions begin to show just who, how and what sort of movement is being made within and across the quadrants. Before I illustrate with an image how I envisage patterns of movement within the FS methodology of structuration model, I wish to discuss how change agents within some of the quadrants can be conceptualised and how (foreign) aid can be productive or counterproductive within the spirit of the FS methodological model.

There will be some overt or covert self-proclaimed change agents who would openly or secretly admit that a given institution is in Q1, 2 or 3 but they have to be in there to change it. I am not here wildly imagining the world of spy agents who remain top secret from certain people. I am describing common African leaders, who routinely want to appear to be the voice of change within 'rotten' institutions. A bit like the former leader of the Liberal Democrats in the UK asking for people to vote for them in the 2015 general elections because, in the event of a hung parliament, they would 'be the brain to Labour government and the heart to a conservative one' (Nick Clegg 2015). It is a matter of trust here but on the African continent, I would be wary of such claims that would, in the long run, give change agents a free pass to navigate through low fear and low self-scrutiny, high fear and low self-scrutiny, and high fear and high self-scrutiny on a regular basis on the pretence that they have to fight the enemy from within.

That, however, does not mean that change agents in Q1, 2 and 3 have to be from outside institutions only. The reality, however, is that former allies have indeed jumped ship, fearlessly to demand greater institutional self-scrutiny from outside the institutions. Whatever one's starting point, genuine change agency in Q1, 2 & 3 involves personal risks, criticism and caricatures. Undeterred, highly patriotic individuals will brave all the threats aimed at increasing fear in the potential change agent. Political parties have been suspended, radio stations closed, phones hacked; these are just some of tactics employed to prevent change.

I have so far described potential movement that could emanate from 'career' agents of change. Some people are career agents in the sense that they choose or aspire to leadership (of any field) as a day-to-day activity. Just because people are in some form of cosy low fear within a baby snake rapport or in high fear either within lion-goat, or nail-dog race rapports, does not mean that they could not be agents of change. According to Giddens, and he is right to say this, 'agency is essentially the capacity to have done otherwise' (Giddens and Pierson 1998, 78). Even at gun point, he argues, people still have the consciousness, or more holistically 'the embodied consciousness', to defy such threats and overcome fear in order to assume their agentic role. The mass protests in the face of repressive live bullets, that we have all witnessed in the history of Africa, is a sign that the real agents of change are not the career agents, even though their charisma and steadfast leadership is valuable, but the people themselves. This may sound like radicalism when viewed one-sidedly, either from a subjective (citizens) or objective (institutions) standpoint. On the contrary, this is radicalism/imperativeness of the recursive-ness of social reality: radical structuration.

The relationship between fear and agency is not one of annihilation but rather of obscurity. Obscurity here can be viewed in the sense of a (covertly) silent presence. Without seeking to encourage anything, there are grounds to affirm a characteristic of agency even in Q1, 2 & 3. This can be detected in the migrant crisis in 2015. It cannot be disputed that the near-to-certain threat of death when crossing the sea from North Africa to southern parts of Europe would be very real to the migrants. It can, however, be explained by understanding that the migrants had been living within a frame of mind where they simply responded to the question 'what is God telling you?' (Q1 key question) or, for the conspiracy theorists, 'did you do what I told you?' (Q2 key question, where migrants are trapped in a lion-goat rapport and on a mission to execute premeditated acts of terrorist in Europe), and others would simply call it a sign of desperation. Behind all that is the subject's capacity to have done otherwise. In the face of death, migrants' agentic fearlessness in embarking on a perilous journey through tumultuous waters and in squalid conditions is clear, and still they are determined to overcome the threat and reconstruct the whole recursive narrative. Replace the migrant scenario with the quest for ntu leadership within a particular institution and then you begin to see that the subjects are the primary un-strippable change agents.

In a non-ntu environment, devoid of the ethical value of integrity, for example, there is commodification of everything, to the point that even agency is thought to be amenable to the lures of the highest bidder. Wiseman (2002) has already talked about the creation of bogus opposition parties. The results of the freest and fairest elections on the continent still depend on handing over huge amounts of money during campaigns to get the most votes, precisely because of the pervasiveness of commodification of subjects' agency. Exiled voices in the diaspora have been noticeably active more recently, thanks to the rapid spread of technology but, while they can have a positive influence, they too are not immune to the phenomenon of commodification of agency.

Anecdotal and yet crucial is the point about commodification, which is often seen as an aspect of life associated with the rise of Western consumerism (Gottdiener 200) and not Africa. While such an assertion can hold as an

162

argument, one still needs to interrogate such assumptions. Focusing on African traditions alone, further research is still required to understand certain narratives around practices such as the paying of a bride price or dowry. Chadwick (1970), for example, makes a convincing case for the functionality of the dowry payment as a symbolic recompense to the bride's family for doing what the man (groom) himself should have done in the upbringing of his now wife. The man, it is hoped, will also be recompensed with children and that is why, in East Africa, for example, the bride price is returned if the woman does not bear children, a practice which is now being challenged by a series of rulings by supreme courts both in Kenya and Uganda. The author also notes the commercialisation or commodification of this partnership with: 'it is discouraging to see a custom misused by parents who have come to regard it as a form of pension in their old age' (ibid 148). Even if this is decried in the strongest term, it can be understood from Weiburst's (1997) categorisation that even if culture is not grasped in its historical nature, it can still be understood in the way that it is interpreted and how it manifests itself in modern times. To return to the thrust of the argument for this publication, the commodification of agency can be seen as a capitalist import but, as I have demonstrated in the foregoing discussion, it can also be seen as a way in which African commodification practices have evolved (perhaps for the wrong reasons).

Does education then help to sharpen up the masses' sense of agency? Yes and no. The purpose of me writing about it, and this book being used and discussed at different community and institutional levels, is an admission that education helps in the realisation of low fear agents. It remains to be seen whether institutions that might be regarded as Q1, 2 & 3 would promote it or not. Resistance can be understood as a way of countering the power to unmark and sharpen agency that a literature like this one, and other initiatives such as aid, as I shall discuss shortly, can have. However, as mentioned earlier, Africa has largely been failed by its educated generation of children, which questions the potential this publication could have for one's resolve to apply its ideas in daily life. At the end of the day, rather than offer a pedagogy of *ntu* leadership (Q4), there is nothing this book or anybody else can do over and above the final decision that leaders must make, in order to be more or less self-scrutinising and unleash potential or condemn generations to further Q 1, 2 & 3 dealings or agents, which have to overcome or give in to fear to demand greater transparency and involvement in the shaping and reshaping of their institutions.

Let us suppose that the above change agents act genuinely to bring about change that reflects all of the Q4 characteristics. Whether they act that way or not, what else can be or has been done on the African continent to ensure that there is movement towards ntu leadership and citizenship within a more prosperous environment? I will characterise some initiatives as 'cosmetic change' (examples are: bogus institutions and creation of wealth and employment that is unfairly distributed), 'forced change' (coups either by power hungry individuals or against an institution that seems to have lost either/or both legality and legitimacy), and 'incremental/developmental change'

Cosmetic change is the opposite of genuine change by genuine actors. During his 2015 three-day state visit to Uganda, the Kenyan president Uhuru Kenyatta had this to say to members of Ugandan parliament: 'In Kenya, we have learnt to accept opposition who should not legitimise government actions but bring legitimate solutions to the country's problems'. Bogus change agents, similar to what Wiseman (2002) alleges to have happened in Mobutu's Zaire and probably a current practice in several African countries where they create puppet opposition parties, can only bring about the change that is the opposite of what President Uhuru Kenyatta alluded to - cosmetic change.

Forced change through military or popular uprising is another category that has been both welcomed, in the case of people rising up against Q3 like practices when President Blaise Compaoré tried to change the constitution, and unwelcomed in

164

Africa, in the case of the 2004 failed coup allegedly involving foreign nationals seeking to depose Equatorial Guinea's leadership. However, as already argued, a non-ntu leadership is concerned with legality rather than legitimacy, which some might argue makes forced change (perhaps after exploring other avenues) a legitimate course of action to bring about *ntu* leadership. That said, a clear outline of tipping points warranting forced change is still lacking in the vision of regional organisations, including the African Union (AU).

Incremental or developmental change is rather tricky, mainly because of the dilemma of having to do business with a leadership that one might think falls squarely within Q1, 2 or 3. Those who see things in black and white would only take extreme views of either conditional involvement, associated with the Western stance on Africa when it demands that some standards of human rights and democracy be met, or unconditional engagement, associated with the Chinese approach. I see the conditions set by the West as similar to the demands of Q4, which is underpinned by a *ntu* ontology. The downside of the Western stance is that they too have backed and collaborated with Q1, 2 and 3 leaders when it suited them, during the cold war for example, and during those years there is hardly anything in the way of infrastructure to show for it. China, on the other hand, a country built on starkly other leadership traditions, is engaged in building infrastructure whose lure might bring some to excuse a possible unscrutinised cooperation with Q1, 2 and 3 leaders, in the hope that such activities will one day emancipate the masses.

With the rise in popularity of 'unregulated' Eurobond loans among African countries, at a time of economic uncertainty for both the Eurozone and China (Kratt 2015), we see the European space adopting the Chinese approach of not tying lending/aid to the commitment to democratic principles, which opens up the possibility that China could one day use the Bretton Wood rhetoric of conditional loans to ensure that the African markets/states do not revert to European 'unregulated' money to fulfil their development and other dreams. One of the many lessons to draw from this is best summed up by the saying 'you cannot give what you haven't got'. It is, therefore, naïve of Africa to expect the West, China, India, Brazil, Russia etc., to model ntu leadership for them. The danger, therefore, is for Africa to fall *willingly* into the same trap they were *forcibly* put into during colonisation. That of accepting to do business in a non-African way (the non-ntu way) only to cry foul later on, saying we were stripped of our African-ness. One voice of authority in this field, who has been calling for trade as the answer, is Dambisa Moyo. I discuss her perspective next.

Aid can be thought to have a developmental impact. There is, however, one articulate critic of aid, who sums it up in the title *Dead Aid* (Moyo 2009). It is possible that such a title would have a negative effect on donors whether they are ordinary people, diaspora or foreign institutions. However, most benefactors would not bear the thought of wasteful generosity or one's help having an adverse effect. Hence, there is a need to consider Dambisa Moyo's argument carefully. I will use two extracts from two of my informants (a member of a diasporan association I call Buzz and a member of a state institution in an African country whom I refer to here as Bizz).

'What I like with our association is that we are in control of our destiny. Sometimes, we collect money, send it back home to build a school here and there and it could take years before government takes up the running of the school' *Buzz*.

'I was shocked as soon as I started working within x institution. There are roads and schools that have been signed off by government as having been built by them and the bills have been picked up by either the state treasury or foreign donors. In reality, nothing was done and most of that money would have gone into people's pockets' *Bizz*.

When you contrast Buzz and Bizz's accounts, it begs the question whether aid is worthwhile. Dambisa Moyo does explain why such corruption practices occur but the examples she advances, which are similar to those of Buzz and Bizz, are

166

discussed in a narrow causational or correlational approach. Hence, aid leads to corruption and, therefore, it is dead. I would argue that there is a wider context to consider and it is possible to imagine that corruption would have been evident in other spheres of life among Africans, and indeed the world over, way before 1944, the year to which the author has traced the origins of aid.

Whether aid feeds into corruption and dependency or not, as argued by Moyo, the author's literature is crucial in highlighting the need for her critics, such as Bill Gates, who would argue that there is nothing wrong in aid that stops poor people from dying of malaria, for example, to realise that the end does not always justify the means and that *ntu* ontology demands for the process to be as dignified as the outcome.

The significant weakness that unravels Moyo's argument, however, is her failure to provide her fictitious Republic of Dongo, which she assumes represents 'all' African states, with some ontological and methodological underpinnings. Where the author attempts to give it some structure, the description is rather chronological, suggesting a linear trajectory from socialism through privatisation to democratisation. It remains an unfinished business, if those historical accounts and the economic trends they displayed are seen outside of the basic sociological characteristics of a social entity such as Dongo. If effort is made to reconstruct the Republic of Dongo, one would struggle to describe it as based on either agency or structure, which is not only un-African but also philosophically and sociologically indefensible. The successes and woes of Africa can only be talked about convincingly from an *ntu* ontology, otherwise known as structuration theory, where there is interdependence of force-beings or structure and agency within a sliding ontological scale of fear (for agents) and self-scrutiny (for structures).

If approached in that manner, the author's next crucial point would have been to advance a coherent methodological approach. Again, if one had to reconstruct the Republic of

Dongo in the light of the FS methodology of structuration, we would not end up with one but four Republics of Dongo, displaying the defining characteristics of Q1, 2, 3 and 4.

With such evidence-based variety, one is then able to begin a rigorous analysis of how aid has or can become dead. Anyone conducting such an analysis must also be forthright with their ontological bias before it emerges to overshadow the argument instead of informing it. In the case of Moyo, her approach that leading to the conclusion of Dead Aid seems to be inspired by an ontological approach that views aid as intrinsically cancerous. I would at this point use a biblical analogy to suggest a non-cancerous way of looking at aid.

'A farmer went out to sow his seed. As he was scattering the seed, some fell along the path (**Q1?**), and the birds came and ate it up. Some fell on rocky places (**Q2?**), where it did not have much soil. It sprang up quickly, because the soil was shallow. But when the sun came up, the plants were scorched, and they withered because they had no root. Other seed fell among thorns (**Q3?**), which grew up and choked the plants. Still other seed fell on good soil (**Q4?**), where it produced a crop—a hundred, sixty or thirty times what was sown. Whoever has ears, let them hear' (Matthew 13).

You can almost predict where I am going with this. Aid, in itself, is not the issue but the ontological and methodological mechanisms of leadership are what make aid work or not. My position does not absolve the farmer from having ulterior motives but to blame it all on aid is rather naïve given the multiplicity of systems, some of which are less favourable to development.

Moyo calls for trade as the solution which again fails to acknowledge that even trade is trapped in the ontological opacity of the methodological quadrants 1, 2 and 3. It is important that the question of imbalance of subsidies that disfavours African farmers is discussed and that Moyo's suggestions are taken into account but the author also fails to see that in some African countries within Q1, 2 and 3, wealth is not only concentrated

168

among a few individuals but the rules of the game are not the same for all citizens. Mobutu once allowed his citizens to extract whatever minerals they wanted but they were not allowed to sell them outside the country, except to designated people. In legally biased environments, those who had the buying power to acquire all the produce, of local farmers for example, would make such individuals the 'real' farmers (mineral dealers), who would then negotiate a 'fair' trade deal with the vast markets of the US and Europe.

The dilemma then is 'can incremental change be feasible in the cases of Q1, 2 and 3?' What does one do in a continent where the triangular patterns of movement, as illustrated by the figure below tend to intensify mainly in Q1, 2 and 3 prompting comments like 'Africa is a scar in the conscience of the world' from the former British prime minister Tony Blair? If you are, like me, a steadfast supporter of African leadership based on Ubuntu as described in Q4 then you are likely to reverse Tony Blair's comment into 'there is a conscience in the scar of the world that is Africa'. That conscience, though not fully manifest, can be brought to bear through the help of the AU and other regional bodies, which need to show vision in their leadership.

The danger here is to think that everything in Africa has gone horribly wrong. There are several examples of Q4 but I will refrain from giving further examples that should be the work of citizens and researchers alike in a constantly evolving African narrative. There is also another danger of becoming complacent and accepting change at a snail's pace when we can make several strides ahead at the same time. The AU of today, in my view, does not give off the signals of a body which not only has *ntu* ideals but is also willing to put in place constraining measures that bring those claiming to be part of it into the fold. In the confusion, it is sending mixed messages about those ideals to its onlookers. An example of this is in appointing some of its leaders who, according to this analysis, could be put under Q1, 2 and 3, as emissaries to resolve conflicts and move institutions, hopefully to Q4. It is true that no one is a saint and people are

169

able to do 'as one says and not as one does' but an organisation such as the AU, among others, needs to reflect on the signals it is sending out and how it appears to legitimise the leadership of those emissaries.

Discipline in an African context is a topic that has not been discussed here. Yet, in a contemporary world, most institutions must have this if they are to deter structures and agents from ever breaking that bond of trust (see Chapter 2). In education, schools that are underperforming can be put under special measures and, in the financial world, credit rating agencies upgrade or downgrade economies representing high risks. With a body beyond reproach, such as the elders, the AU's Peace and Security Council, for example, can receive unbiased analysis of a country's progress towards *ntu* leadership. Such data and recommendation would then help the AU to decide whether a certain leadership is of Q1, 2 or 3. That assessment and decision should then come with legally binding powers for the AU and restrictions for the outside world (the West and China), who might think of doing (bilateral) business that would only become Dead Aid. Let me be clear that such a position does not apply to your regular person, who sees a business opportunity to invest here and there. However, the legal powers of the AU, for example, have to be within a time limit leading to exclusion or other appropriate and necessary consequences, unlike the ineffective consultative and advisory body of the Pan African parliament and the voluntary African Peer Review Mechanism within Nepad, which are non-compliant (Uzodike 2010).

This may sound familiar to those well versed in Dambisa Moyo's argument where the author calls for a market-based relationship between Africa and the West. It is a relationship that is not without risks, to which the author attempts to advance some mitigating factors. While some of her ideas are worth considering, others, to put it politely, are in need of review. To reassure creditors in the event of an African country defaulting, the author recommends that other African countries, such as South Africa, act as a guarantor. She illustrates this with an example, which brings her optimistically to conclude that 'South Africa is effectively underwriting the risk of the whole continent' (Moyo 2009, 95). It is unthinkable that one country's tax payers can be expected to bear the brunt of other countries under Q1, 2 and 3 styles of leadership. But in so doing, the one who fits the bill can claim to have more of a say in matters of national and regional interest. Therefore, the repercussions of Moyo's arguments could be that, as Africa is weaned off its old dependency on the West (and China?), new dependencies on emerging African regional powers, such as South Africa (South), Nigeria (West), Chad (central), Kenya (East) and Ethiopia (Horn) (Saunders 2014) would take over. This does not only increase the suspicion some African states and citizens have towards these economic powers that run regional institutions to their advantage, it also brings us back to the argument made in Chapter 1, where the call for a return to African values seems to advocate for the replacement of colonial non-ntu structures with new non-ntu African structures. This fails to grasp a people's sociological worldview.

Moyo's argument, in my view, can be awarded some merit only if it is built on a leadership ontological rating, such as the one being proposed here. In the midst of *The New Scramble for Africa*, Carmody (2011) has asked whether Africans can unscramble Africa, before suggesting that governments adopt a strategic approach to foreign investment. Discussing intra-African trade, Akinkugbe (2010:132) has also called for 'policy and structural reforms so as to diversify their export basket. They will also need to rationalise and strengthen the various institutions that they have created to enhance such efforts'. The FS model, I believe, represents a solidly argued and authentic African (but also instrumental, see Zoogah and Nkomo 2013, in 'a brief mapping of the field' section) ontological and methodological grounding of governance, political culture and various other aspects of life such as tribalism etc.

However, there are some well-rehearsed fears that would lead some to find the body I am calling for objectionable. There are three main concerns that can be termed as the *sovereignty*, *division* and *politics* arguments to which I will now turn.

The *sovereignty* argument defends a nation's inalienable right for self-determination. This is a question of self-identity that is agreeable, especially when you have had a history of inhumane colonial domination. The Dutch philosopher Burach Spinoza is well known for his monism, which is the conception that 'there is and can be only one substance' (Charlton 1981). When sovereignty is defended in absolute terms and a country sees itself as a monad, oppressive regimes can use the same argument not to defend self-determination but self-suicide. Self-determination, therefore, cannot be taken as the right to continuously dehumanise others under the pretext of national sovereignty. Regional and international bodies, such as the Security Council, need to reflect on this issue in order to shape international law accordingly. The irony of monism, embedded in the sovereignty argument, is also that it is contradicted when the same absolutely sovereign institutions employ the separation argument.

The *separation* argument is built on the fear of a divided Africa if the kind of body I am calling for is adopted. Here, the monad called the state seems to have dilated to become a continent whose unity must now be preserved absolutely. But that is as far as it can go. The same logic that would enable a view of the world as a monad, united around certain values, is often discarded and perhaps rightly or wrongly viewed as neo-colonialism. My analysis has shown that, unless Africans want to disown Ubuntu, we are in rather similar territory with those non-Africans who draw inspiration from Giddens' structuration theory. The separation argument is also based on a misunderstanding of the words 'union' (through Pan Africanism and the African Union) and 'interdependence' (through Ubuntu). I would argue that the creation of various bodies (unity organisations) was never an end in itself but a means to a far greater project of realising *ntu* ontology (interdependence of force-beings Q4).

172

The *politics* argument points to the various difficulties of ever making such a body work, given the conflicting interests in a complex world. How and where do you find men and women of integrity to head this body? 53 African countries would all want to have a stake in it. The body will be infiltrated by people with other agendas. These are just some of the political difficulties that may be used, perhaps in good faith, to question and discard the proposal as unworkable. This, I think, is rather defeatist. If good things can never work, then it is an indictment that those national institutions still 'functioning' are the opposite of the Q4 'Ubuntu' body I am proposing; all the more reason why such a body needs to work. The *Barza* example, used as case study 4, worked and then failed precisely because Q4 bodies are never static. They can be infiltrated by people with Q1, 2 and 3 motives, which only goes to prove that movement away from Q4 (see figure below) is possible, if and when the body ceases to be self-scrutinising in the face of low fear agents.

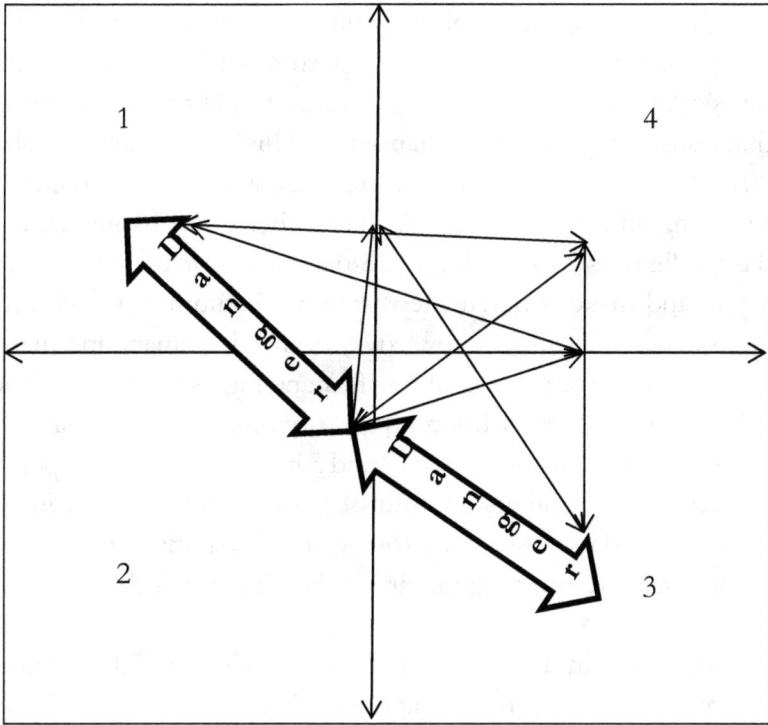

Conclusion

Rather than summarise a summative chapter, I will end with a brief discussion of the above figure and what I call the *Singapore conundrum*.

Given the Ubuntu and non-Ubuntu interests pulling the African leadership arena in differing directions, the above straight or zigzag or circular or spiral line movements within a triangular pattern 'represent an opportunity for negotiation and renegotiation in a never-ending stream of political manoeuvring that constitutes everyday organisational life' (Hatch and Cunlife 2013:233). In such a political arena of agents and structures assuming and assuring trust to each other (see Chapter 2), the danger lines as shown above are named so for their failure to aspire and make concrete steps towards Ubuntu (Q4), with its approach to education, knowledge, legality, legitimacy and many others, within the context of low fear and high self-scrutiny. The other lines in their Q4-bound trajectory (not the reverse or only transiting through Q4 but Q1, 2 and 3 bound) are more hopeful. However, in an endless contour of poor leadership that can no longer defend itself using the sovereignty, separation and politics arguments, the only argument left is what I call the *Singapore conundrum*.

Reporting in The New York Times, Mydans (2015) marks the passing of the first Singaporean Prime Minister Lee Kuan Yew with the following description: 'his leadership was criticised for suppressing freedom, but the formula succeeded. Singapore became an admired international business and financial centre'. The *Singapore conundrum* does raise a lot of questions in the minds of various African agents, elites running various institutions, and even partners who have to deal with non-Ubuntu styles of leadership. 'If we can have a dictator who loves his or her country', 'what matters is that I have a vision for my country and I will not listen to anyone until I have achieved that vision' and 'he/she is not as bad as…so maybe we can work with him/her' are all possible scenarios being contemplated by various parties

175

whose agency is obscured but figuring out which is the best of the three worst cases scenarios - Q1, 2 and 3. It is even casually hinted at Mydans' article that 'if they had three Lee Kuan Yews in Africa, that continent wouldn't be in such a bad state'.

The first response is to remind the reader of the need to banish thoughts that would perpetuate the idea evoked earlier that 'Africa is the scar in the conscience of the world' (Tony Blair). Instead, use Q4 (FS model) to believe and accept nothing less than what 'this conscience (Q4) in the scar is urging you to do'. That said, a logical argument to prove that even the *Singapore Conundrum* is self-destructive is warranted.

With some leaders having done more than 10 years' (dis)service, not to mention 30+, the Messiah for an equivalent African Singapore would have been a reality already. Not only is it dangerous to accord someone a free ride with no self-scrutiny and/or biased high scrutiny but also, if it hasn't already happened in the case of 10+ years of Q1, 2 and 3 leadership, my suspicion is that it would never happen and whoever uses that as an argument is motivated by similar Q1, 2 and 3 ethics (egoism). Africa's endless conflicts are also further proof that Q1, 2 and 3 cannot bring about a truly reconciled society. Another point is also that the Singapore example, which falls into Q1, 2 and 3 is un-African and, as such, it falls short of the true principles of Ubuntu (low fear and high self-scrutiny).

Those inclined to resuscitate (extreme) structuralism would point to Singapore as an example where subjects do not play a part in the formation of social reality. However, with the FS methodology of Ubuntu (structuration) in mind, such tyranny of either structuralism or subjectivism is truly obsolete, as even the *Singapore conundrum* would always happen within the context of either low or high fearing agents. Even the argument that leaders or leadership has a naturally objective and independent existence is only a partial narrative, in the face of those who believe in the complexity of forces (including agents, albeit passively in some instances) at play in the exercising of leadership (Dubrin 2013). What the *Singapore conundrum* does instead is highlight a

176

contradiction mentioned earlier where I argued that some African leaders and scholars have, for years, reclaimed their Black/African identity from a fixed oppressor and not against oppression, regardless of its source. The final point I wish to make is through inviting the reader to look again at Singapore and ask whether it was/is really a success. Mydans' report also goes on to highlight other sinister characteristics of such an approach that left people feeling jittery and obliged to follow dictates; encouraging a particular race to copulate more to deal with the drop in population growth and the opposition winning nearly 40% of the country's popular support is indicative of the fact that agents wanted to end their passive role and hold institutions to account.

Taken in its simplest form before becoming a topic of discussion in university lecture rooms or a tool for further research and an emancipatory framework for leadership activities around ethnicity, body, economics, aid, journalism, judiciary, policing etc., the FS methodology of *ntu*/structuration is a question of producing the best script for leadership and citizenship in both secular and non-secular fields. I would, therefore, urge policy makers to ensure that the ideas discussed here are adapted and become part of the curriculum, where parents, social/youth workers, teachers and students etc. familiarise themselves with the essence of the FS model, in line with structuration theory/*ntu's* way of life. Rather than being seen as a concept solely to assess institutions or citizens' commitment to the practice of structuration theory or Ubuntu, it should also be viewed as a way of life that can be learned through training. The title '*Trapped?*' (Elonga Mboyo 2016a) goes some way to meeting those goals.

References

Abrahamsen, R. (2003). African studies and the postcolonial challenge, In *African Affairs,* 102, 189-210.

Acedo, C. (2012). World-class education: a response to global challenges. In *Prospects,* 42, 335-336

Akinkugbe, O. (2010). Intra-African trade and economic development, In Adar G K., Juma K.M., and Miti N.K., *The State of Africa, Parameters and Legacies of Governance and issue areas,* Pretoria: African Institute of South Africa 119-134

Akokpari, J. (2010). Politics and governance in Africa, In Adar G K., Juma K.M., and Miti N.K., *The State of Africa, Parameters and Legacies of Governance and issue areas,* Pretoria: African Institute of South Africa. 69-85

Albatch, G. P. (1971). Education and neo-colonialism: a note. In *Comparative Education Review.* 15, 2, 237-239.

Albatch, P. G. (2007). Empires of knowledge and development. In Albatch P. G. and Balan, J. (Eds.). *World class World-wide: Transforming Research Universities in Asia and Latin America,* 1-28. Baltimore: John Hopkins University Press.

Aliber, M. (2003). 'Chronic poverty in South Africa: Incidence, causes and policies. In *World Development,* 31, 3, 473-490

Allafrica.com (1st November 2012). *Students Seek Ban on Politicians' Children Schooling Abroad,* Al Bawada (Middle East)

Amonoo-Neizer, H. E. (1998). Universities in Africa: The need for adaptation, transformation, reformation and revitalisation. In *Higher Education Policy,* 11, 301-309.

Anderson, B. (1991). *Imagined Communities,* London: Verso.

Anonymous (2010). West Africa Hosts Untapped Mineral Wealth, In *Engineering and Mining Journal,* 54-59

Anta Diop, C. (1962). *The Cultural Unity of Negro Africa,* Paris: Presence Africaine

Appadurai, A. (2009). The shifting ground from which we speak. In Fenway J. and Fahey J.(eds), *Globalising the Research Imagination*, 41-552. London: Routledge

Arazi, N. (2009). Cultural research management in Africa: challenges, dangers and opportunities, In *Azania: Archaeological Research in Africa*, 44, 1, 95-106.

Archer M (2002) Realism and the problem of agency. *The Journal of Critical Realism* 5(1): 11–20.

Archer, M. (1995). *Realist Social Theory: The morphogenetic approach.* Cambridge: Cambridge University Press.

Arthur, J. (1991). Development and crime in Africa: a test of modernization theory, In *Journal of Criminal Justice*, 19, 6, 499-513.

Axel, K.B. (1998). Disembodiment and the total body, In *Third Text*, 12, 44, 3-16

Ayittey, B.N.G. (2010) Traditional institutions and the state of accountability in Africa, In *Social Research*, 77, 4, 1183-1210

Bachelard, Y. J. (2010). The anglo-leasing corruption scandal in Kenya: the politics of international and domestic pressures and counter-pressures, In *Review of African Political Economy*, 37, 124, 187-200.

Ball, J. S. (2008). Performativity, privatisation, professionals and the state, In Cunningham, B. (Ed). *Exploring Professionalism*, 50-72. London: Institute of Education, University of London.

Bangura, A.K. (2008a). The politics of the struggle to resolve the conflict in Uganda: Westerners pushing their legal approach versus Ugandans insisting on their Mato Oput, In *Journal of Pan African Studies*, 2, 5, 142-178

Banks, M. (1996). *Ethnicity: Anthropological Constructions*, London: Routledge

Barley, S.R and Tolbert P.S. (1997). *Institutionalisation and structuration: Studying the links between actions and institutions*, Retrieved 06/09/2015 from Cornell University, ILR School site: http://digitalcommons.ilr.cornell.edu/articles/130/

Bartkey, L.S. (2008). Foucault, feminism, and the modernisation of patriarchal power, In Malacrida C and Low J (eds) *Sociology of the Body: A Reader*, Oxford University Press 21-27

Bates, E.A. (2007). Wearing the T-shirt: an exploration of the ideological underpinnings of visual representations of the African body with HIV or AIDS, In *African Journal of AIDS Research*, 6, 1, 67-78, DOI: 10.2989/16085900709490400

Bauman, Z. (2006). *Liquid Fear*, Cambridge: Polity

Beck, U. Giddens, A. and Lash, S. (1994). *Reflexive modernisation: Politics, tradition and aesthetics in the modern social order*. Stanford, CA: Stanford University Press.

Benneh, G. (2002). Research management in Africa, In *Higher Education Policy*, 15, 249-262

Berkeley, B. (2001) Race, tribe and power in the heart of Africa, In *World Policy Journal*, 18, 1, 79-87

Bertilsson, M. (1984). Review article: the theory of structuration: prospects and problems. In *Acta Sociologica*. 27, 4, 339-353

Beso, A., Bollaert, L., Curvale, B., Jensen, H. T., Harvey, L., and EmmiHelle (Eds.). (2008). *Implementing and Using Quality Assurance: Strategy and practice. A Selection of papers from the 2nd European quality assurance forum:* EUA.

Bhambra, K. G., Shilliam, R. and Orrells, D., (2014). Contesting imperial epistemologies: introduction. In *Journal of Historical sociology*, 27, 3, 293-301

Blaikie, N. (2000). *Designing Social Research*, Cambridge: Polity

Bloom, E.D., Canning, D. and Sevilla, J. (2004). The effect of health on economic growth: A production function approach, In *World Development*, 32, 1, 1-13

Bolden, R., Petroc, G., Gosling, J., and Bryman, A. (2009). Leadership in higher education: facts, fictions and futures – introduction to the special issue, In *Leadership*, 5, 3, 291-298

Boudon, R. (1998). Limitations of rational choice theory, In *Chicago Journals*, 103, 3:817-828.

Bourdieu, P. (1958). *La sociologie de l'Algérie*. Paris : Presses universitaires de France

Bourdieu, P. (1984). *Distinction: A Social Critique of the Judgement of Taste*. London: Routledge.

Bourdieu, P. (1984). *Homo Academicus*. Stamford, Ca: Stanford University Press

Bourdieu, P. (1990). *The Logic of Practice*, trans. Richard Nice, Cambridge: Polity

Bourdieu, P. (1993). *The Field of Cultural Production*. Cambridge, UK: Polity Press.

Bourdieu, P. and Passeron, J-C. (1990) *Reproduction in Education, Society and Culture*. London, Sage.

Brewer, D.J., Gates, S. M., and Goldman, C. A. (2002). *Pursuit of Prestige: Strategy and competition in the US Higher Education*. New Brunswick, NJ: Transaction Publishers.

Bristow, F.W. (2002). Are Kant's categories subjective? In *The Review of Metaphysics*, 55, 3, 551-580.

Brock, C. (2012). Perspectives on the contribution of higher education to education as a humanitarian response. In *Journal of Comparative and International Education*, 1, 1, 13-22.

Brock, C. and Alexiadou, N. (2013). *Education Around the World, A comparative Introduction*, London: Bloomsbuty

Brown, C. (1984). *The Art of Coalition-Building: A Guide for Community Leaders*. New York: American Jewish Committee.

Burrell, G. and Morgan, G. (1979). *Sociological Paradigms and Organisational Analysis*. Aldershot: Gower.

Bush, T. (2011). *Theories of educational leadership and management*, 4th ed. London, Sage

Caldwell, C.J., Orubuloye, O.I., and Caldwell P., (1997). Male and female circumcision in Africa, from a regional to a specific Nigerian examination, In *Soc. Sci. Med.*, 44, 8, 1181-1193

Carmody, P. (2011). *The New scramble for Africa*, Cambridge: Polity

Carr, D. (2003). Philosophy and the meaning of education, In *Theory and Research in Education*, 1, 2, 195-212

Carroll, K.K. (2014). An introduction to African-Centered sociology: worldview, epistemology, and social theory, In *Critical Sociology*, 40, 2, 257-270

Castle, S. (2011) As nationalism surges in Europe, Poland begins bloc presidency, In *New York Times*

Chadwick, P.F. (1970). Some ideas concerning the origin of dowry in East Africa, In *The Journal of Modern African Studies*, 8, 1, 143-149

Chandler, B. (2013). The subjectivity of habitus, In *Journal for the Theory of Social Behaviour*, 43, 4, 469-491

Charlton, W. (1981) Spinoza's monism, In *The Philosophical Review*, 90, 4, 503-529

Cheville, J. (2005). Confronting the problem of the body, In *International Journal of Qualitative Studies in Education*, 18, 1, 85-107.

Christian, J.P. (2013) Darfur-ground zero for Africa's crises of identity: Psychohistoriography of tribes in conflict, In *African Security*, 6, 1, 1-37

Cilliers, P. (2005). Complexity, deconstruction and relativism. In *Theory, Culture and Society*, 22, 5, 255-267. Doi: 10.1177/0263276405058052

Clark, J.F. (2002). *The African Stakes of the Congo War*. Basingstoke: Palgrave MacMillan.

Clark, P. (2008). Ethnicity, leadership and conflict mediation in Eastern Democratic Republic of Congo: the case of the Barza inter-communautaire, In *Journal of Eastern African Studies*, 2, 1, 1-17.

Clark, P. (28Nov-4th Dec 2013). The price of admission. In *Times Higher Education*, 2, 129, 36-41

Cohen, W.D. and Odhiambo A. E.S. (1992). *Burying SM*, London: James Currey

Commentary (2004). The politics of trust, In *The Political Quarterly Publishing*, 99-101.

Coombs, P. and Ahmed, M. (1974). *Attacking Rural Poverty, how Non-formal Education Can Help*. Baltimore: Johns Hopkins University Press.
183

Cooper, N. (2006) Colonial humanism in the 1930s, the case of Andrée Viollis, In *French Cultural Studies*, 17, 2, 189-205

Creswell, W. J. (2007). *Qualitative Enquiry and Research Design, Choosing among Five Approaches*, 2nd ed., London: Sage.

Cunningham, B. (2008). Critical incidents in professional life and learning. In Cunningham, B. (Ed). *Exploring Professionalism*, 161-189. London: Institute of Education, University of London.

Curtis, N. (2006). Justice, In *Theory, Culture and Society*, 23, 2-3, 454-455

De Herdt, T., Titeca, K. and Wagemakers, I. (2012). Make schools, not war? Donors' rewriting of the social contract in the DRC, In *Development and Policy Review*, 30, 6, 681-701.

Dei, J. G. (2014). The African scholar in the Western academy, In *Journal of Black Studies*, 45, 3, 167-179.

Dei, J.G. (1994). Afrocentricity: A cornerstone of pedagogy, In *Anthropology and Education Quarterly*, 25, 1, 3-28

Denzin, K. N and Lincoln, Y. (2008). Critical methodologies and indigenous inquiry, In Denzin, N.K, Lincoln, Y. and Smith, L. T. (Eds.), *Handbook of Critical and Indigenous Methodologies*, 1-20. London: Sage.

Denzin, N. (1990). Reading rational choice theory, In *Rationality and Society*, 2, 2, 172-189.

Dixon, J.V. (1977). African-oriented and Euro-American-oriented world views: research methodologies and economics, In *The Review of Black Political Economy*. 7, 2, 119-156

Drubin, J.A. (2013). *Leadership: Research Findings, Practice and Skills*, 7th Ed. South-West, OH, Erin Joyner.

Du Bois, W.E.B. (1973). *The Education of Black People; Ten Critiques, 1906-1960*. Amherst: University of Massachusetts Press.

Durkheim, E. (1952). *Suicide: A Study in Sociology*. London: Routledge

Durkheim, E. (1975b). Individualism and the intellectuals, trans S Lukes and J Lukes. In: Pickering WSF (ed.) *Durkheim on*

Religion: A Selection of Readings with Bibliographies, pp. 59–73. London: Routledge & Kegan Paul

Echterhoff, G., Higgins, T. and Levine, J. (2009). Shared reality, experiencing commonality with others' inner states about the world. In *Perspectives on Psychological Science*. 4, 5, 496-521.

El-Badawy, et al., (Oct. 2015). *Inside the Jihadi Mind, Understanding Ideology and Propaganda*, Centre on Religion and Geopolitics, the Tony Blair Faith Foundation

Elonga Mboyo, J.P (2015a) *Africa through Structuration Theory-ntu*, Langaa, Cameroon

Elonga Mboyo, J.P. (2015b). *The Unexpected Homecoming*. London: Austin Macauley

Elonga Mboyo, J.P. (2016a). *Trapped? Empowering communities to face modern day vulnerabilities of exclusion, extremism, radicalisation, terrorism, grooming, addiction and bullying*. United Kingdom: Vetmaf

Eskay, M., Onu V.C., Igbo J.N., Obiyo, N., and Ugwuanyi, L. (2012) Disability within the African culture, In *US-China Education Review*, 4, 473-484.

Fafunwa, A. B. (1975). *History of Education in Nigeria*. London: George Allen & Co.

Fafunwa, A. B. (1976). *New Perspective in African Education*. London: Macmillan

Foster, M. (1997). *Black Teachers on Teaching*. New York: The New Press.

Foucault, M. (1972). *The Archaeology of Knowledge*. London: Tavistock.

Freidson, E. (2001). *Professionalism: the third logic*. Cambridge: Polity.

Freire, P. (1970). *Pedagogy of the Oppressed*, London: Penguin Books.

Fu, B-J., Zhuang, X-L., Jiang, G-B., Shi, J. and Lu, Y-H. (2007). Environmental problems and challenges in China. In *Environmental Science and Technology*, 41, 22, 7597-7602.

Fuchs C. (2003). Structuration theory and self-organisation, In *System Practice and Action Research*, 16, 2, 133-167.

Fullwiley, D. (2015). Race, genes, power, In *British Journal of Sociology*, 66, 1, 36-45

Gambetta, D. (2000). 'Can we trust trust?', in Gambetta, D. (ed.). *Trust: Making and Breaking Cooperative Relations*, pp. 213–27. Oxford: University of Oxford.

Geertz, C. (1973). *The Interpretation of Cultures*. London: Hutchinson.

Gibson L J. (2004). Does truth lead to reconciliation? Testing the causal assumptions of South African truth and reconciliation process. In *American Journal of Political Science*. 48, 2, 201-217.

Giddens, A. (1979). *The Central Problems of Social Theory*. London: Macmillan

Giddens, A. (1984). *The Constitution of Society*. Cambridge: Polity.

Giddens, A. (2001). *Sociology*, 4th ed. Cambridge: Polity

Giddens, A. (2002). *Run Away World: How Globalisation is Shaping our Lives*. London: Profile

Giddens, A., and Pierson, C. (1998). *Conversations with Antony Giddens: Making Sense of Modernity*. Cambridge: polity.

Gitau M.T., Micklesfield, K.L, Pettifor M.J., and Norris, A.S., (2014). Eating attitudes, body image satisfaction and self-esteem of South African Black and White male adolescents and their perception of female body silhouettes, In *Journal of Child & Adolescent Mental Health*, 26, 3, 193-205.

Glaser, G.B., and Strauss, L.A. (1999). *The Discovery of Grounded Theory: Strategies for Qualitative Research*. New Brunswick: Aldine Transaction

Goffee, R., and Jones, G., (1998). *The Character of a Corporation*. New York: Harper Business

Goleman, D., Boyatzis, R., and McKee, A. (2013). *Primal Leadership: Unleashing, the power of emotional intelligence*. Boston, Massachusetts, Havard Business Review Press.

Gottdiener, M. (2000). *New Forms of Consumption: Consumers, Culture and Commodification*. Oxford: Rowman and Littlefield

Greenfield, T.B. (1986). The decline and fall of science in educational administration, In *Interchange*, 17, 2, 57-80

Grenfell, M. (2008). Interest, in Grenfell M. (ed). *Pierre Bourdier: key concepts*. 153-170. Durham : Acumen.

Grix, J. (2002). Introducing Students to the Generic Terminology of Social Research, In *Politics*, 22, 3, 175-186.

Guardian (The) (2016) School pupls arrested in Burundi for defacing photos president, accessed at https://www.theguardian.com/world/2016/jun/07/schoo l-pupils-arrested-burundi-defacing-photos-president-pierre-nkurunziza?CMP=share_btn_fb

Guile, D. and Lucas, N. (1999). Thinking initial teacher education and professional development in further education: Towards the learning professional. In Green, A. and Lucas, N. (Eds). *FE and Lifelong Learning: Realigning the sector for the twenty-first century*. London: London Institute of Education.

Gyekye, K. (1995). *An Essay on African Philosophical Thought: The Akan Conceptual Scheme*, Philadelphia, PA: Temple University Press.

Handy, C., (1978) *The Gods of Management*. London: Pan Books

Hargreaves, A. (2003). *Teaching in the Knowledge Society: Education in the age of insecurity*. Maidenhead: Open University Press.

Harrison, R. (1979). Understanding your Organisation's Character. Havard Business Review, 57, 5, 119-128

Hatch, J.M., and Cunliffe, L.A. (2013). *Organisation Theory: Modern, Symbolic, and Postmodern Perspectives* (3rd Ed). Oxford, Oxford University Press

Heidegger, M. (1954). *On the Essence of Truth*. Frankfurt: Klostermann

Higgs, P. (2012) African philosophy and the decolonisation of education in Africa: some critical reflections, In *Educational Philosophy and Theory*, 44, 2, 37-55.

Hodge, S. (2012). Guest editorial, *Perspectives in Public Health*. 132, 1, 16

Hofstede, G. (1991) *Cultures and Organisations*, London: McGraw-Hill

Howlett, M. and Weelstead, A. (2011). Policy Analysts in the Bureaucracy Revisited: The Nature of Professional Policy Work in Contemporary Government, In *Politics and Policy*, 39, 4, 613-633.

Hughes, J. and Sharrock, W. (1997). *The Philosophy of Social Research*, 3rd ed., London and New York: Longman.

Ibelema, M. (2014). Tribal fixation and Africa's otherness: changes and resilience in news coverage, In Journalism and Communication Monographs, 16, 3, 162-217

Jeongwoo, L. (2013). Creating world-class universities: Implications for developing countries. In *Prospects*, 43, 233-249.

Johnson W. (2004). Never the same river. In *Proquest Education Journals*. 61, 3, 381-390.

Jonasson, J.T. (2008). *Inventing Tomorrow's University. Who is to Take the Lead?* Bologna: The Magna Carta Observatory.

Jones, R. M. and Karsten H. (2008). Gidden's structuration theory and information system research, In *MIS Quarterly*, 32, 1, 127-157.

Journal of Black Studies, 33, 399-449.

Kasanda, A. (2016) Africa through structuration theory – ntu (Book review). *Modern Africa: Politics, History, and Society*, 4, 1

Keskin, T. (2014). Sociology of Africa: A non-orientalist approach to African, Africa and black studies, In *Critical Sociology*, 40, 2, 187-202

Kimoyo, J.P. (2008). *Un Génocide Populaire*, Editions Karthala

Kirk, P and Bolden, R. *African leadership: insights, meanings and connotations*, Proceedings and the leadership and management studies in Sub-Saharan Africa (June 2006)

Kittle, B. (2000). Institutional advertising in higher education. In *Journal of Marketing for Higher Education*, 9, 4, 37-52.

Kratt, E. Eurobonds: Africa's new patronage machine, *Global Risks Insights* http://globalriskinsights.com/2015/12/eurobonds-africas-new-patronage-machine/ accessed on 22/12/2015

Laplante, J. (2004). *Pouvoir Guérir: Médecines autochtones et humanitaires*. Québec : Presses de l'université Laval.

Larson, M. S. (1977). *The Rise of Professionalism*. California: University of California Press.

Lash, S. (1994). Reflexivity and its doubles : structure, aesthetics, community, 110-173, In Beck, U., Giddens, A., and Lash, S., *Reflexive Modernisation*, Stafford, CA: Stafford University Press

Leonardi, C. (2004). Traditional accountability and modern governance in Africa (conference paper). In *African Affairs*, 103/413, 661-663.

Letseka, M. (2000). African Philosophy and Educational Discourse, In Higgs, P., Vakalisa, N. C. G., Mda, T. V. & Assie-Lumumba, N. T. (eds), AfricanVoices in Education (Cape Town, Juta).

Letseka, M. (2013). Anchoring Ubuntu morality. In *Mediterranean Journal of Social Sciences*. 4, 3, 351-359.

Levering, B. (2007). Epistemological issues in phenomenological research : How authoritative are people's accounts of their own perceptions ?, 215-226, In Bridges, B. and Smith, R., (Eds), *Philosophy, Methodology and Educational Research*, Oxford, UK: Blackwell Publishing

Littrell, F.R., Wu, H.N., Nkomo, S., Wanasika, I., Howel, J., and Dorfman, P. (2013). Pan-Sub-Saharan African managerial leadership and values of Ubuntu, In Lituchy R. T. et al, *Management in Africa, Macro and Micro Perspectives*, London: Routledge 232-248.

Lomotey, K. (1994). African-American principals: Bureaucrat/administrators and ethno-humanists. In M. J. Shujaa (Ed.), *Too Much Schooling, Too Little Education: A paradox in African American life* (pp. 203-219). Trenton, NJ: Africa World Press.

Loyal, S. (2009). The French in Algeria, Algerians in France: Bourdieu, colonialism, and migration. In *The sociological Review*, 57, 3, 406-427.

Lunt, I. (2008). Ethical issues in professional life. In Cunningham, B. (Ed), 73-98 *Exploring Professionalism*. London: Institute of Education, University of London.

Lupton, D. (1998). *The Emotional Self.* London: Sage

Luyaluka, K.L. (2016). An essay on naturalised epistemology of African indigenous knowledge, In *Journal of Black Studies*, 1-28 DOI: 10.1177/0021934716646043

Madzokere, N. and Machingura, F. (2015). True and false prophets/esses in the light of prophets/esses and wondres in Zimbabwe, In *Journal of Critical Southern Studies*, 3, 53-71

Maffesoli, M. (1996). *The Time of the Tribes: The Decline of Individualism in Mass Society.* London: Sage

Mandela, N. (18th July, 2007) Nelson Mandela and Desmond Tutu announce the Elders, theelders.org

Marshall, C. and Rossman, S.B. (2011). *Designing Qualitative Research*, 5th ed. Thousand Oaks, C.A: Sage.

Marshall, R. (1991). Power in the name of Jesus, In *Review of African Political Economy*, 52, 21-37

Martin, J. (2002) *Organisation Culture: Mapping the terrain*, Newbury Park, CA: Sage

Mason, J. (1996). *Qualitative Researching.* London: Sage.

Mazama, A (2001) The Afrocentric paradigm: contours and definitions, In *Journal of Black Studies*, 31, 387-405

Mbeki, M. T. (2001). African Renaissance and Traditional Leadership, In *Presidents and Prime Ministers*, 10, 4, 15

Mbigi, L. (1997). *Ubuntu : The African Dream in Management.* Randburg, South African: Knowledge Resources.

Mbiti, J. S. (1969). *African Religions and Philosophy.* London, Heinemann.

McCormark, B., Kitson, A., Harvey G., Rycroft-Malone, J., Titchen, A., and Seers K. (2002). Getting evidence into practice: the meaning of practice. In *Journal of Advanced Nursing*, 38, 1, 94-104.

McKenna, T. (2011). Hegelian dialectics, In *Critique: Journal of Socialist Theory*. 39, 1, 155-172.

McRoy, I. and Gibbs, P. (2009). Leading change in higher education. In *Educational Management, Administration and Leadership*, 37, 5, 687-704.

Mentan, T. (2009). *Democratizing or Reconfiguring Predatory Autocracy? Myths and Realities in Africa Today*, Cameroon: Langaa RPCIG

Mentan, T. (2015). *Unmasking Social Science Imperialism: Globalization theory as a phase of academic colonialism*, Cameroon: Langaa RPCIG

Merizon, J. (1997). Transformation theory out of context. In *Adult Education Quarterly*. 48, 1, 60-62. DOI: 10.1177/074171369704800105.

Miti, N.K, Juma, K.M., and Adar, G.K. (2010). Confronting Africa's development challenge, In In Adar g k., juma K.M., and miti n.K., *The State of Africa, Parameters and Legacies of Governance and issue areas*, Pretoria: African Institute of South Africa 245-252

Mizrahi, T. and Rosenthal, B.B. (2001). Complexities of coalition building; leaders' successes, strategies, struggles and solutions, In *Social Work*, 46, 1, 63-78

Mokonzi, G. (2010). *DRC: Effective Delivery of Public Services in the Education Sector*. Johannesburg: Open Society Institute for Southern Africa

Molefi, A and Kariamu, A. (eds) (1990). *African Culture: Rhythm and Unity*. Trenton, NJ: Africa World Press

Molefi, A. (1987) *The Afrocentric Idea*, Philadelphia, PA: Temple University Press

Montesquieu: *Lettres persanes*, 1721. [Reprint published by GF-Flammarion, Paris, 1964].

Moyo, D. (2009). *Dead Aid*, London: Penguin Books

Mukonyora, I. (2007). Globalisation and the university in Africa. In *Social Dynamics: A Journal of African Studies*. 33, 1, 221-223.

Murrell, P. (2002). *African-centered Pedagogy: Developing schools of achievement for African American children*. Albany: State University of New York Press.

Mwaba, K and Roman N.V. (2009). Body image satisfaction among a sample of black female South African students, In *Scientific Journal publishers*, 37, 7, 905-909

Mydans, S. (March 22, 2015). Lee Kuan Yew, Founding father and First Premier of Singapore, Dies at 91, in *The New York Times*, accessed at http://www.nytimes.com/2015/03/23/world/asia/lee-kuan-yew-founding-father-and-first-premier-of-singapore-dies-at-91.html?_r=0

Myers, L.J. (1987). The deep structure of culture: the relevance of traditional African culture in contemporary times, In *Journal of Black Studies*, 18, 1, 72-85

Myers, R. A., Omorodion, F. I., lsenalumhe, A. E. and Akenzua, G. I. (1985). Circumcision: its nature and practice, In *Social Science & Medicine* 21,581-588.

Naidoo, P and Bacela, P.A. (2012). Power and energy in Africa: a wealth of possibilities, In *IEEE Power and Energy Magazine*, 67-70

Neal, S. (2008). Feared and revered: media representations of the racialised and gendered bodies-a case study, In Malacrida C and Low J (eds) *Sociology of the Body: A Reader*, Oxford University Press 284-289

Newland, K. and Patrick, E. (2004). *Beyond Remittances: The role of Diaspora in poverty reduction in their countries of origin*, Migration Policy Institute.

Nishida, T. (2008). *Situated Knowledge Management for Primordial Knowledge Model*, international conference on informatics education and research for knowledge-circulating society. IEEE

Nwabueze, B. (1984). *Constitutional Democracy in Africa*, Spectrum books

O'Neil, O. (2002). *A Question of Trust. The BBC Reith Lectures 2002*. Cambridge: Cambridge University Press.

Obiakor, E. F. (2004). Building patriotic African leadership through African-centred education, In *Journal of Black Studies*. 34, 3, 402-420.

OECD. (2008). The Democratic Republic of Congo. In *African Economic Outlook*, 241-255

Ogundele, O.J.K.,and Hassan, A.R. (2013). Challenge of Ethics, In Lituchy R. T. et al, *Management in Africa, Macro and Micro Perspectives*, London: Routledge 112-132

Okpewho, I. (1977). Principles of traditional African art, In *The Journal of Easthetics and Art Criticism*, 35, 3, 301-313

Olukoshi, A. (2006). African scholars and African studies. In *Development in Practice*, 16, 6, 533-544.

Onwudiwe, E and Ibelema, M. (2003). *Afro-optimism: Perspectives in African advances*. Westport, CT: Praeger.

Pandey, R. (2005). Desire and disgust: meditation on the impure body in medieval Japanese narratives, In *Monumenta Nipponica*, 60, 2, 195-234.

Papastephanou, M. (2001). Reformulating reason for philosophy of education, In *Educational Theory*, 51, 3, 293-313

Perry, L.J., Mesch, D. and Paarlberg, L. (2006). Motivating employees in a new governance era: The performance paradigm revisited. In *Public Administration Review*, 66, 4, 505-514.

Pillay, P. (2010). *Linking Higher Education and Economic Development*. South Africa, African Minds Publishers

Polyani, M., (1966). *The Tacit Dimension*. London: Routledge.

Pring, R. (1994). 'Liberal Education and Vocational Preparation', in R. Barrow and P. White (eds) *Beyond Liberal Education: Essays in Honour of Paul H. Hirst*, pp. 49–78. London: Routledge.

Pring, R. (1995). *Closing the Gap: Liberal Education and Vocational Education*. London: Hodder and Stoughton.

Proctor, N.R. (2008). The destruction of 'lives not worth living', In Malacrida C and Low J (eds) *Sociology of the Body: A Reader*, Oxford University Press 92-99

Puri, S. (2004). *The Caribbean Postcolonial: Social Equality, Post-Nationalism, and Cultural Hybridity*. New York: Palgrave MacMillan.

Quan, H.L.T and Willoughby-Herard, T. (2013). Black ontology, radical scholarship and freedom, In *African Identities*, 11, 2, 109-116.

Rabaka, R. (2003). W. E. B. Du Bois's evolving Africana philosophy of education. In

Ray, C. (2008) How the word 'tribe' stereotypes Africa, In *New Africa*, 471, 8-9

Razack, H.S. (2008). Gendered racial violence and spacialised justice: the murder of Pamela George, In Malacrida C and Low J (eds) *Sociology of the Body: A Reader*, Oxford University Press 298-304

Reagan, T. (2005). *Non-Western Educational Traditions: Indegenous approaches to educational thought and practice*, 3rd ed., London: Lawrence Erlbaum Associates

Ribbins, P. and Gunter, H. (2002). Mapping leadership studies in education: towards a typology of knowledge domains, In *Education Management & Administration*, 30, 4, 359-385

Riessman, K.C. (2008). *Narrative Methods for the Human Sciences*. London: Sage

Robertson, L. S. (2012). World-class higher education (for whom?). In *Prospects*

Rogowski, R. (1974). *Rational Legitimacy*, Princeton: Princeton University Press

Rosenthal, B. and Mizrahi, T. (1994). *Strategic partnerships: How to Create and Maintain Interorganisational Collaborations and Coalitions*. New York: Education Centre for Community Organisation.

Sapienza, P., Toldra-Simats, A. and Zingales, L. (2013). Understanding trust, In *The Economic Journal*, 123, 1313-1332.

Saunders, C. (2014) South Africa and Africa, In *Annals AAPSS*, 652, 222-237

Schegloff, A. E. (1997). Whose text? Whose context? In *Discourse and Society*. 8, 2, 165-187.
DOI: 10.1177/0957926597008002002

Schein, E. (1984). Coming to a new awareness of organisational culture, In *Sloan Management Review*, 25, 2, 3-16

Sewell, H. W. (1992). A theory of structure: duality, agency and transformation, In *Chicago Journals*, 98, 1: 1-29

Shilling, C. (2001). Embodiment, experience and theory: in defence of the sociological tradition, In *The Editorial Board of the Sociological Review*, 49, 3, 327-344

Shilling, C. (2008). The body in Sociology, In Malacrida C and Low J (eds) *Sociology of the Body: A Reader*, Oxford University Press 7-13.

Sikes, P. (2006). Decolonising research and methodologies: indigenous people and cross-cultural contexts. In *Pedagogy, Culture & Society*, 14, 3, 349-358.

Sikes, P. (2013). Working together for critical research ethics. In *Compare: A Journal of Comparative and International Education*, 43, 4, 516-536.

Slaughter, B.J., (2012). Thoughts on educational leadership, In Gallagher et al, *Urban education, A Model for Leadership and Policy*, London: Routledge 85-87

Smaje, C. (1997). Not just a social construct: theorising race and ethnicity, In *Sociology*, 31, 2, 307-327.

Smart, N. (2008). *World Philosophies*. London: Routledge

Smeulers, A. and Hoex, L. (2010). Studying the micro-dynamics of the Rwandan genocide, In *Brit. J. Criminol* 50, 435-454

Smith, J., Flowers, P., and Larkin, M. (2009). *Interpretative Phenomenological Analysis: Theory, method and research*. London: Sage.

Smith, L. T. (1999). *Decolonizing Methodologies: Research and indigenous peoples*. London: Zed Books.

Stacey, R.D. (2000). *Complex Responsive Processes in Organizations: Learning and knowledge creation (complexity and emergence in organizations)*. London: Routledge

Stephan, M.W. (1992) Measuring political legitimacy, In *The American Political Science Review*, 86, 1, 149-166

Stone, L. (2007). US graduate study in educational research: From methodology to potential totalization (265-282), In Bridges, D. and Smith, R. (eds). *Philosophy, Methodology and Educational Research*, Oxford, Blackwell Publishing.

Stones, R. (2005). *Structuration Theory*. Basingstoke: Palgrave Macmillan Routledge.

Teferra, D. and Albatch, P. G. (2004). African higher education: Challenges for the 21st century. In *Higher Education*, 47, 21-50.

Tempels, P. (1959). *Bantu: Philosophy*. Paris: Presence Africaine.

Thomson, A. (2004). *An Introduction to African Politics*. London: Routledge.

Titeca, K. and De Herdt, T. (2011). Real governance beyond the 'failed-sate': Negotiating education in the Democratic Republic of the Congo. In *Africa Affairs*, 110, 439, 213-231.

Tobert, W.R. (2001). The practice of action enquiry. In Reason P. & Bradbury H. (eds). *Handbook of Action Research*, 250-260. London: Sage

Tonkiss, F. (2012). Discourse analysis, 405-423. In Clive S. (ed). *Researching Society and Culture*, 3rd ed., London: Sage.

Torbert, W.R. (1999). The distinctive questions development action inquiry asks. In *Management Learning*, 30, 189-206.

Torres De Souza, A.M and Agostini, M. (2012). Body Marks, Pots, and Pipes: Some Correlations between African Scarifications and Pottery Decoration in Eighteenth- and Nineteenth-Century Brazil, In *Historical Archaeology*, 46, 3, 102-123

Tsand, W.K.E., and Williams N.J. (2012). Generalisation and induction: misconceptions, clarifications, and a clarification of induction, In *MIS Quarterly*, 36, 3, 729-748.

Tutu, D. (2010). Ubuntu: the essence of humanity, In *Amnesty International*, 37, 4, 23

Tyldesley, M. (2013). Postmodernity, aesthetics and tribalism: An interview with Michel Maffesoli, In *Theory, Culture and Society*, 30, 3, 108-113.

Udokang, L.E. (2014). Traditional ethics and social order: A study in African philosophy, In *Cross-Cultural Communication*, 10, 6, 226-270

Unesco. (2010). *Annuaire Statistique de l'enseignement Supérieur et Universitaire : Année Académique 2008-2009.*

Université Laval. (2014). Certificat en Enseignement Professional et Technique. Accessed February 5, 2014 at http://www.fse.ulaval.ca/prog/c-ept-ept/bref/

Uzodike, U. (2010). Pan-African governance architecture: prospects and future, In Adar G K., Juma K.M., and Miti N.K., *The State of Africa, Parameters and Legacies of Governance and issue areas,* Pretoria: African Institute of South Africa 87-102

Van de Veen, R. and Preece, J. (2005). Poverty reduction and adult education, beyond basic education. In *International Journal of Lifelong Education.* 24 5, 381-391.

Vertigans, S. (2007). Beyond the fringe? Radicalisation within the American far-right, In *Totalitarian Movements and Political Religions,* 8, 3-4, 641-659

Wang, Y., Xu, L., and Jones, B.J. (2013). The effect of the Chinese cultural revolution and great leap forward on the prevalence of myopia. In *European Journal of Epistemology,* 28,12, 1001-1004.

Weiburst, P. (1989). Tradition as process: creating contemporary tradition in a rural Norwegian school and community, In *International Journal of Qualitative Studies in Education* 2, 2, 107-122

Whitty, G. (2008). Changing modes of teacher professionalism: Traditional, managerial, collaborative and democratic, In Cunningham, B. (Ed). *Exploring Professionalism,*28-59. London: Institute of Education, University of London.

Wilson, A. (1992). *Awakening the Natural Genius of Black Children.* New York: African World InfoSystem.

Wiseman, J.A. (2002). The movement towards democracy: global, continental and state perspectives, In Wiseman, J.A (ed). *Democracy and Political Change in Sub-Saharan Africa,* London, Routledge. 1-10

World Bank (2015). *Unemployment, Youth Total* (% of total labor force ages 15-24) (modeledILOestimate)http://data.worldbank.org/indicator /SL.UEM.1524.ZS/countries/1W-NG-ZA?display=graph, accessed on 02/08/2015.

Wright, M.M. (2010). Black in time: exploring new ontologies, new dimensions, new epistemologies of the African Diaspora, In *Transforming Anthropology*, 18, 1, 70-73

Zambeta, E. (2002). Modernisation of educational governance in Greece: from state control to state steering, In *European Educational Research Journal*, 1, 637-655.

Zoogah, B.D. and Nkomo S. (2013). Management research in Africa, past, present and future, In Lituchy R. T. et al, *Management in Africa, Macro and Micro Perspectives*, London: Routledge. 9-31

Index

201